TWAYNE'S WORLD AUTHORS SERIES
A Survey of the World's Literature

Sylvia E. Bowman, Indiana University
GENERAL EDITOR

NEW ZEALAND

Joseph Jones, University of Texas
EDITOR

D'Arcy Cresswell

(TWAS 205)

TWAYNE'S WORLD AUTHORS SERIES (TWAS)

The purpose of TWAS is to survey the major writers — novelists, dramatists, historians, poets, philosophers, and critics — of the nations of the world. Among the national literatures covered are those of Australia, Canada, China, Eastern Europe, France, Germany, Greece, India, Italy, Japan, Latin America, the Netherlands, New Zealand, Poland, Russia, Scandinavia, Spain, and the African nations, as well as Hebrew, Yiddish, and Latin Classical literature. This survey is complemented by Twayne's United States Authors Series and English Authors Series.

The intent of each volume in these series is to present a critical-analytical study of the works of the writer; to include biographical and historical material that may be necessary for understanding, appreciation, and critical appraisal of the writer; and to present all material in clear, concise English — but not to vitiate the scholarly content of the work by doing so.

D'Arcy Cresswell

By RODERICK FINLAYSON

Twayne Publishers, Inc.　　::　　New York

For HELEN SHAW,
also a poet
who generously helped and always encouraged

Preface

This study of a modern poet is unusual in that the writings of D'Arcy Cresswell are unlikely to be available to the reader of this work, and much of the poet's philosophy, on which he based his poetry, remains unpublished. It is, indeed, part of my purpose to show the importance of Cresswell's view of the modern world, and to hope to arouse enough interest in his work, both the poetry and the other writings, to justify its presentation anew.

Because the texts will thus not be familiar to the reader, as with most modern poets they would be, lengthy quotations from the various works will be necessary. In the Introduction it is my intention to show the environment in which Cresswell grew to manhood, and to comment on the periodic journeyings throughout his life between New Zealand, his native country, and England, his spiritual parent; between the New World and the Old; between the Hades of the Southern Hemisphere and the lost Paradise of the Northern. The Chronology will be a guide to these and to the few other journeys that Cresswell made. In regard to his travels from New Zealand to England, the reader will note that they occurred at periods of about seven years to begin with, as Cresswell points out in his autobiography, although in later years the war interrupted that frequency. What was the reason for that seemingly restless shuttling to and fro?

Unusual too, for a poet, is the fact that Cresswell's prose writings are more numerous and tend to be better known than his verse, and due to the perfection of their style they tend to be more highly regarded, and even to earn for him the title of philosopher. While Cresswell rejected that title, he himself, in one place in his autobiography, exclaims of his *Thesis* on the nature of poetry, "I should almost call it my philosophy!" It will be necessary for me to show how intimately related those two forms of expression become; how dependent the verse became on the hard ground-clearing work of the lucid and coolly reasoned prose.

Generally, my plan is to relate Cresswell's chief poetical works to roughly four periods of his life. After the overall review of the Introduction the first period will introduce the early verse in its setting of *The Poet's Progress*. In this early period, although the verse may be unsure, Cresswell writes of his life and his progress with an authority and a sense of direction that was never to falter.

In the second period we shall study the essay on *Modern Poetry and the Ideal, Lyttelton Harbour,* a sequence of thirty-nine sonnets, and *Eena Deena Dynamo,* an essay in which Cresswell announces the downfall of modern science. In this period the poet attains maturity in both experience and expression after seven years of Herculean labors in the Hades of the modern world.

This will naturally lead to a consideration of *The Forest,* a three-act play in blank verse. We shall also learn more of Cresswell's views on life and the arts contained in *Present Without Leave,* which is the continuation of his autobiography. These works may be counted the fruits of his maturity. In this third period we have both Cresswell's judgments on poetry and on the modern world, and a revelation of times to come.

The fourth period will include various sonnets, satires, and other poems, and an examination of the long poem *The Voyage of the Hurunui.* This poem, his last of any length, presents us with both strange difficulties and some interesting deductions.

Besides summing up, and a glance at how Cresswell appeared to his contemporaries, the Conclusion will be devoted to the yet unpublished but most remarkable work named *A Thesis on the Mechanism of Spirit or Poetic Intention in Man.*

Finally let me mention a particular difficulty, for the reader as much as for the interpreter of Cresswell's works. It will soon be evident that it was Cresswell's mission, as he saw it, to condemn not only most modern poetry and all the assumptions on which that poetry relies, but also the whole modern world of science and its foundations, not even hesitating to denounce the Copernican universe as a falsehood and figment of licentious reason. This is a stand so unusual, and a challenge so sweet, that I must be allowed quite lengthy quotations from the unpublished *Thesis,* for it is my intention to show what justification there is for Cresswell's attitude.

Besides those due to all of Cresswell's publishers, of whom full details are given in the Bibliography, acknowledgments are also due to Mr. David Cresswell for permission to quote from letters and unpublished poems, and to Messrs. Ormond Wilson and Denis Glover, Cresswell's literary trustees, for making available such papers, as also to the authorities of the Turnbull Library, Wellington, and the Auckland Public Library which house collections of Cresswell's letters and papers. Special thanks to Helen Shaw (Mrs. Hofmann) for allowing perusal of a great number of Cresswell's letters, many not to be found in public collections.

Contents

Chronology

1896 Walter D'Arcy Cresswell born January 22, at Christchurch, New Zealand, son of W. J. Cresswell, barrister and solicitor.

1912 Left school at Christ's College, Christchurch.

1913 Entered office of Collins and Harmon, Architects, Christchurch.

1914 First voyage to England. Architect's assistant in London until the outbreak of World War I, when he joined the Middlesex Regiment.

1915 Wounded in action in France and discharged.

1916 Joined New Zealand Engineers and served in France until the end of the war.

1919 Returned to New Zealand.

1921 Second voyage to England, leaving Wellington in April.

1921 Six months in Cologne, Germany.

1922 Took part, in Wales, in the General Election campaign of November of that year.

1923 Five months in Spain and Portugal.

1925 Married the Freda of the sonnets. One son, David.

1927 *Poems 1921–1927* published by Wells Gardner, London.

1928 Returned to Christchurch early in the year.
Third voyage to England near the end of the year.

1930 *The Poet's Progress* published by Faber and Faber, London.

1931 *Poems 1924–1931* published by The Bodley Head, London.
Returned to Christchurch later in the year.

1932 Left Christchurch for Auckland and before the end of 1933 was living at Castor Bay, Auckland. Began giving radio talks on various aspects of poetry.

1934 *Modern Poetry and the Ideal* published by The Unicorn Press, Auckland.

1936 *Lyttelton Harbour* published by The Unicorn Press, and *Eena Deena Dynamo* by the Caxton Press, Christchurch.

1938   Fourth voyage to England, sailing from Wellington toward the end of July.

1939   Began his residence at The Cottage, St. John's Wood, London. *Present Without Leave*, the second part of his autobiography, published by Cassell, London.

1940   Some years of "war work," various broadcasts and lectures to troops.

1942   In July was confirmed in St. Paul's Cathedral by the then Bishop of London.

1948   *Margaret McMillan — A Memoir* published by Hutchinson's.

1950   A short visit to New Zealand on the motor ship *Hurunui*, returning on the same ship later in the year, his fifth voyage to England.

1951   In July began employment as night-watchman in a government building in London, an employment which continued until the time of his death.

1952   *The Forest* published by The Pelorus Press, Auckland.

1956   *The Voyage of the Hurunui* published by the Caxton Press, Christchurch.

1960   Died February 21 at London.

CHAPTER 1

The End of a World

I *Is the Modern World Dead?*

I was born in Eighteen-ninety-six,
A thousand years ago,
Shortly before the sun went down
And it began to snow.

IN the year 1871 Ernest Rutherford was born; in 1896, D'Arcy Cresswell—both of them New Zealanders, one a scientist, the other a poet. Early in the twentieth century Rutherford "split the atom" and thus became responsible, even though indirectly, for the destruction in a new way of the substance of a city or two before the middle of that century. But Cresswell has destroyed, in essence, the entire modern world. Only that world does not yet realize the fact of its death; for that end has been effected not grossly as with a bomb, but cleanly and precisely with the swift keen sword of the spirit, leaving the world like those characters in our childhood stories who were delicately pierced by a rapier or whose necks were severed by a razor-sharp blade, and continued to believe themselves unharmed until a cough or a sneeze betrayed them.

The very foundations of the modern world, all for which and by which it can be said to have any existence in fact, were publicly destroyed by Cresswell when in 1936, after five years or more of prodigious labor in the refining of his intellectual weapon, he published his *Eena Deena Dynamo, or The Downfall of Modern Science*. Now, with the passing of each decade since then, we can surely see more awfully the abyss into which, at the indiscreet cough of a politician or sneeze of a scientist, our severed world

may topple. Two New Zealanders: between them they may be
said to be responsible for the end of *our* world.

And if the world is hardly yet aware of its fate, it is still less
aware of the words of its denouncer. Let us then consider this
man and his works which were the fruit of an unshaken belief
in his mission; in what he would call his truthful search. For,
he insists, "the search for truth" (which saying presupposes that
there is no truth in us) "must give place to the truthful search,
which is the supernatural in Nature as sought and found through
the senses by the spirit of Man."[1] As, in another age, at the end
of an earlier world, Saint Paul proclaimed to the spiritually dead
Romans, "What can be known about God is perfectly plain [to
men] since God himself has made it plain. Ever since he created
the world his everlasting power and deity—however invisible—
have been there for the mind to see in the things he has made."[2]
If one but looks, with one's eyes open, Cresswell would add.

II   *A New Earth*

Walter D'Arcy Cresswell was born in the South Island province
of Canterbury in New Zealand. At that time, 1896, and in that
place practically nothing that marks the modern world as such
was to be found. In that half-wild countryside of boundless
plains and few small towns, overlooked by the awful snowy
heights of the Southern Alps, there were no cars, no airplanes,
practically no knowledge of electricity. The telephone was still
a novelty, and there were of course none of those other gadgets
that almost govern men's minds today, no motion pictures, radio,
or television. Farming largely followed the ways of yeoman
England adapted to vaster spaces; and life in the small towns,
and even in the infant cities, was a mixture of Victorian England
and the American West; candles and oil lamps, horses and bug-
gies, the simple and homemade kinds of amusement. Only the
beginning of steam railways and the arrival of steamships showed
that the material changes in society were creeping in; the material
changes which, slowly at first, inevitably followed the subtle
changes in men's thinking that shaped the modern world.

"In the early days," as they say in New Zealand—that is, in
pioneering times up to the turn of the century—in a strange and
harsh new environment all had to be managed by brave initiative

and originality. The arts were not neglected, though; indeed, the new environment tended to bring them, for a while, a freshness and new liveliness. This can be seen in the charm of many early sketches and watercolors. Most of them were the works not of professional or studio artists, but of explorers, surveyors, soldiers, or missionaries, portraying the people and places they saw on their travels, and the actions they shared in the wars with the native inhabitants. Much of the architecture of those days, especially the country houses and the churches, shows the same charm of unpretentious honesty of construction and reliance on proportion and simple line. And everywhere, together with the simplicity and absence of sophistication, there was a buoyancy of spirit and upsurge of energy and the excitement of adventure on all sides.

Indeed, the settlers and their children shared this naturalness and spontaneity. Their whole environment was conducive, because of its stern and unrelenting character, to honesty with one's self and freedom from the artificial and the sophisticated. Into that new world the pioneer settlers brought the elements of their homeland culture—the Bible, the latest volume of the poems of Tennyson, the novels of Dickens. And that prophet and censor of the New World, Emerson, found his way into their homes too, to admonish and correct the rest.

And all the while, as Cresswell points out, Nature was acting anew on the hearts, the character, the speech—the poetry, that is, of a people. So that it seemed for a time that all this freshness and originality were not only to endure but to lead in time to new heights of art and expression and freedom of spirit. And Cresswell, a child of that environment, felt sure that his was to be the voice to proclaim both his country's rejection of old traditions and its growing greatness in all that was new—as Whitman had proclaimed America's.

Even in childhood Cresswell had intimations that he was destined to serve the Muse of poetry and to be her trusted messenger. He recalls how as a boy he was at a private school for three years on a wild part of Cook's Strait.

It was a fitting nursery for a poet, a little bay by the sea, and so much of flat land as the enclosing mountains allowed, a world of forest and streams and sea-shore where we roamed at will, and not another person to be met with in months but our little community, wherein I had already discovered myself to be something singular, although I was only ten years old. I had never seen Nature before, in all her wildness, being reared in the city; but I knew her, and what she intended for me, at first sight. Here those ambitions formed in my infancy to which I have been faithful (and to nothing else) ever since. This is what I referred to . . . in *Lyttelton Harbour* when I wrote,

> Where first thy forests were endear'd to me
> In regions of my childhood, long before,
> I stood, my Country, on a promont'ry
> Beside Cook's stormy strait, whose current tore
> Thy wilds in two. And in the ocean's roar
> And bright'ning sun I only thought of ye,
> Ye works of Nature! whose command I bore,
> Even as a child, your messenger to be.[3]

III   *Era of Change*

If only Cresswell and his countrymen had been left to their bright new world! But there, as in America, all that freshness and freedom did not last; as indeed no part of the modern world can enjoy a dispensation apart from the rest. Even in distant and isolated New Zealand exciting changes came, not creeping but crowding in. The changes began in 1882 with the introduction of that ingenious scientific novelty: refrigeration. In that year this invention was applied to the holds of the fast new steamships, and now the produce of New Zealand's new grasslands, huge cargoes of meat and butter, could be shipped overseas "frozen in a state of suspended decay . . . as required by those who control markets and money: a feat that was acclaimed by the settlers as the solution of all their problems and the foundation of the country's future greatness. But in reality no other single act of modern sorcery has been so destructive of our soil, our health, and our social structure." So wrote a critical New Zealander.[4]

Cresswell portrays this turning point in New Zealand's history in the following words:

. . . now a great shout of progress arose; the forests were everywhere set alight, and the ground sown and fenced and stocked while the stumps of the trees were yet smoking. Shiploads of settlers poured into the country, and soon the steamship and railway came to assist and enrich them. . . . Not content with settling the flat lands and accessible ranges, in their frenzy they laid bare even the steepest and most inaccessible mountains. . . . On this account many parts of their islands are now barely inhabited deserts, their streams barren shingle, their birds no more, their waterfalls mute. Thus that mirror of Nature was cracked, the most flawless and heavenly the eyes of men ever beheld on earth. The great bulk of men are monsters, whom freedom makes drunken, whom profit alone attracts. For the profit that came of all this was immense. This, then, was when they learnt to be wise and just and to make laws. This was when the clerks and officials took control of the country. This was democracy![5]

Having as children enjoyed a country fresh and unscarred by industrialization, its mills and slums, New Zealanders of Cresswell's generation had a glimpse of a paradise which could not last. Before Cresswell was fifteen years old the automobile was beginning to churn through the mud of New Zealand's country roads, flying machines had taken off from New Zealand cow paddocks, and the growing cities were beginning to twinkle, if not to blaze, with electric light. The motion picture was ready to project Chaplin's capers before the delighted gaze of New Zealand children, speechless messages by "wireless" circled the earth—and New Zealand's Rutherford began his electrical bombardment of matter. In a year or two he would "split the atom," and the floodgates would open for all the roaring inventions of the next half century, and the coming anguish of an atomic age.

An exciting time and an exciting world for any boy of fifteen. Cresswell was a boy of spirit and, like others, he welcomed that challenging new world. "At that time," he writes in his autobiography, "I was sunk in material things." But even so he was destined for poetry, and his excitement turned to verse. Like Whitman in America's earlier days he began to celebrate material achievements in his verse, and had few, if any, doubts that he was writing great poetry. He saw World War I chiefly as a break, a setback to his country's inevitable progress, a waste of its young manhood. Soon after that war he wrote *The Ghosts of Foam*. In this poem, later to be rewritten as an ode to the resurrection of life, the idea of love and resurrection struggles against the idea of futility and waste, and only a cry to renounce old tradition sounds clearly.

Of the wind's working
With tonic, untainted breath
Unhindered centuries of sun and feeding rains
We have built our perfect plains,
I and my sisters, Australia and Canada
And the New World's mother magnificent,
                    America!
Not for pageantries of death
And laws built of backward looking
But for Life's last, finest chance
Faced and adoring to the day . . . [6]

That was no doubt written about the time that, having used
the outbreak of war as an excuse to escape from bondage to the
profession of architecture, Cresswell was setting out to conquer
London in the role of the great Colonial poet. His friend, C. E.
Carrington, describes his appearance in England on his return
after the war. "The style was aggressive-colonial; his passion for
New Zealand, not yet thwarted by unfriendly criticism, burst out
and flowered in breeches and cowboy hats and a whiff of atmos-
phere from the great wide spaces."[7] He had clearly stated his aims
before leaving New Zealand: ". . . to advance my design of found-
ing my poetry on the traditions, customs and scenery of my
native land."

Because he was a poet, a person more sensitive to every subtle
influence and its growing effects, doubts regarding the truth of
what had once seemed certain now arose in his mind. For soon,
in the climate and soil of New Zealand, so kind to the seeds of
the new ideas as to every other imported weed and pest, inventions and their effects multiplied. These sudden departures from
the traditional and time-tested methods led to great material gain
and the ability to import, besides the necessary and the desirable,
a steady flow of the tawdry, the trashy, and the expendable. Those
living by this increasing trading activity prospered and soon
controlled government, both local and central. Not one of these
had any doubt that this kind of progress would continue. The
faults that quickly appeared, and often became glaring like the
erosion of their hill country and the disease of their cattle, could,
so they assured themselves, soon be remedied by further doses of
science and technology. Utopianism always has been dear to the
New Zealander; and to none more dear than to his huckstering

governments. But the evil inherent in the modern world began to be made plain, to the poet at least, if not to many of his fellow countrymen, until in his heart all previous values were reversed, and he was soon to redefine his concept of the nature of poetry.

Alas! nature is not the goddess of art; but these two, nature and art, are one and the same. As trees come to flower and fruit, so do men. Both nature and art look to a higher God, who can be known but not named. Nowadays there are many who believe that the nature that surrounds us . . . is the perfect original of art; but I hold it is the spirit or harmony of nature that is meant, by which we give expression, by means of analogy, to the spirit or harmony within ourselves, which would otherwise be silent. And this is art, this harmony within ourselves.[8]

A little later he had this to say:

I wrote [much] on the beauties of matter, of which art in no wise consists; or when I looked around with pride on the arena of progress and science, with no knowledge of Fate . . . . But now I dealt with experience in some degree . . . and out of experience alone proceeds that spirit of harmony of which I spoke, which, being breathed as it were, by analogy, into natural forms, a true poem or picture or work of marble or music results.[9]

So we see how far he has traveled, and toward what goal.

Not that he found these truths held publicly in England. He found them only within himself, and the fashionable versifiers of London were to him empty. He did not say they were empty; he found their verse said it for them. And from such verse, no matter how publicly acclaimed, he recoiled as much as from his own once admired great epics of Colonial progress and natural grandeur. He was led to see that poetry partakes of two natures which he called the historic or passive and the private or active. By this he means that the historic nature is a tradition that was once active but is now passive, but the private nature is the energy that makes a man. To this last only Colonial and American poetry inclines too greatly, and is shallow and bad. Yet such energy is the first need of a poet, and this energy modern English poets lack, relying on a dying tradition alone; and this lack is disguised by a desperate originality so as not to seem what it is,

an outworn habit. Cresswell goes on to say that the poets of
newer lands may yet, like energetic bees removed to an alien
countryside, find the wild flowers they need, from which a true
taste will gather that by which and for which we must live. But
those who go by tradition alone are only drones, and bring
nothing to feed our hunger, but will themselves perish when the
winter comes. This, he says, was what he meant when he wrote:

O England! why do you hasten to fall and forget your spring?
Like the leaves that hurry down from the trees in the autumn,
To whirl away over the earth with the following wind,
To lead the way for the year's load of snow,
Which is Death that follows forever the marching summer of life,
Having now only the weak sun of remembered song,
Only cities that are shrouds, only poets that are tombs![10]

IV   *The Poet Grows Up*

At least twice in *The Poet's Progress* Cresswell tells of the
coming of his clearer, maturer vision of the nature of poetry. In
England again, after his travels through Spain and Portugal, he
wondered if he would ever return to his native land.

But now the time was at hand when the thought of returning concerned me less and less, and was nearly extinguished at last; when
the opinion of progress I had, which was based on those parts, and the
worship of flaunted and naked nature engrossed me no more; and
when, above all, I learnt how poetry is based on a painful experience
of life, which was thrust on me soon and reversed all my views. Yet
before this occurred I was warned in a wonderful vision what poetry
was, and had a glimpse of that world where darkness and light are
the forms and shadows of spirits, and hills and ravines the haunts of
satyrs and gods.[11]

And again, alone in his poor lodgings in London,

I was reading Keats in my room, as I had not done for years, when on
a sudden I felt overpowered by his voice. I sat dazed and still, while
slowly the world within me turned upside-down. On the one hand the
surroundings of which my mind was king, the scenery I had rigged,
before which I would act my life, sank out of sight; while on the other
hand that fresh and living world arose in which I am the least inhabi-

tant there is, and I heard all the poets I knew of singing like larks. I shut myself up for some days, while that singing continued, to which I listened entranced . . . . When at last I went out, there was nothing the same, but all was new to my eyes, while the influence of ancient things was a cloud by day and a pillar of fire by night.[12]

And when, a few years later, he did return to New Zealand all there was new to his eyes too, as though he came back a different man, which indeed he did. Now it was more than distaste for machines and inventions that aroused his criticism, it was the character of his fellow countrymen changed by those inventions and the ideas on which they were based. Noting that with the New Zealanders the Feast of the Resurrection takes place in the autumn, he commented that this seeming confusion is of no account because there is no public, and almost no "private," religion among them. Neither is there any regard for free speech, nor any talent for justice. To disagree or to challenge, whether directly or indirectly, they regard as a sign of moral evil, so that few ever venture to do so. "Truly a man needs be dainty to do well amongst them," Cresswell observes. "You might suppose the sea never cast up a stink on their coasts."[13]

He further commented that, with no political talent, they have a great desire to be governed, lest they be thought savages. Consequently, towards almost any variation from the mediocre norm they are narrow and jealous, and cruel in their laws, "neither relaxing those laws which torment a minority nor minding the imposition of those which the majority disobey as they please. So that their notion of what is wrong and what is merely unlawful is determined by the numbers of those who may be concerned . . ."[14]

But Cresswell's ability to appreciate a people's virtues in spite of their weaknesses can be seen in the following statement:

In New Zealand the feminine and sentimental are supposedly confined to the sex in which these attributes are thought to be most becoming —so are the masculine and insensitive. Even in respect of infancy this is popularly thought to be the case, and the least hesitation or confusion on the part of Nature in the matter is apt to infuriate the beholders, and may even set the law and the police force in motion. Manhood and womanhood—hand in hand these stark extremes scour the ranges and explore the beaches without the least human variation in sight to teach them anything better. . . . But the New Zealanders have the saving and promising capacity of knowing, and admitting, a thing when they see it. Too often they don't see it; but by seeing a little they come in time to know something, and are thus the opposites of those decadent intellectuals in more civilised countries who see everything and know nothing.[15]

Likewise he noted that in spite of the fact that they defer in all things to their women, "who requite this attention by debauching their stomach with sickly and factitious foods," they are normally strong and active and have great natural qualities, such as honesty, courage, and endurance, and are at their best in the face of disaster. "In short, their failings are such that enlightenment may remove, while their virtues another people might long in vain to acquire."[16]

Yes, but were Cresswell alive today, he would remark how true his more pessimistic predictions have become. In place of a public religion, the New Zealanders now have public idolatries among them, the most widespread being perhaps the worship of rugby football (allied, in their butter producing center, to adoration of the Golden Calf), to which they even sacrifice their moral principles. He would see freedom falling ever more under intolerance, and would observe his country's once healthily growing independence now blighted by a timid new deferring to whichever Great Power they wish to strike a bargain with in order to protect them from the results of their follies. In regard to petty mischief he would hear the cry of "Vandalism!" raised by those in high places who themselves shatter the mirror of Nature, "the most flawless and heavenly the eyes of men ever beheld on earth." Vandals are not found among the lowly and merely ignorant, but among those blinded by power, the arrogant and the unenlightened.

All these things Cresswell foresaw and warned his countrymen against during his lifetime; but even as early as 1930 he had published enough in the Christchurch newspaper that he wrote for to earn the enmity and the intolerant abuse of many in his native city. When, earlier, he had written that New Zealand was but another and smaller America, he had been comparing his country's pioneering days with America's, and showing that they both shared that freshness, freedom, and spontaneity we spoke of. But now he saw that New Zealand was truly becoming a little America. However, the words he now used to describe his onetime "mother magnificent," were very different: "mechanical, soulless, shifty, overweening, callous America." In the next paragraph of the essay (on the decline of taste in the modern world) that contained that judgment, he softened its harshness.

Yet if America so far is evil, ignorant, and without shame, it cannot be denied that Americans have benefited from the change of air, in naturalness, spontaneity, and that most fruitful honesty, honesty with one's self. . . . The youngest generation of New Zealanders is already showing those excellent if quite uncultured characteristics. . . . I confess there is also the same American materialism here, and love of money. But there are even worse things, we find, more fatal to a people and to poetry, than materialism and money. Evil as these are, yet man has only to abandon them. There is nothing worse than sophistication, a wit that has lost comparison with life, a politeness beyond our means. From such in himself man cannot flee. [17]

If, as Cresswell maintained, because of the unparalleled debauchery of the age, there should soon be some heaven-sent sign of the rebirth of poetry, a fresh shoot of grass amid the growth of rank incoherent materialism, he at first looked in vain to find it. At length he looked to where he had least expected to find it, to "unprincipled, materialistic America," and discovered amid the endless catalogs and the American chauvinism of Walt Whitman some fresh green shoots. After pages of the usual—"I show that size is only development./ Are you the President?" etc.—Cresswell came to the line, "I am he that walks with the tender and growing night." And he paused amazed. And again, "I depart as air, I shake my white locks at the runaway sun." And this: "Long and long has the grass been growing,/ Long and long has the rain been falling,/ Long has the globe been rolling round." "To alert ears," Cresswell wrote, "the peculiar personal majesty and mystery of these lines has not been heard in our language since Byron. . . . Indeed Whitman's freer form gives to those lines an even remoter and fresher appearance, like the Psalms or like Sappho." [18]

He welcomes, too, the "rustic furrow" of Emerson's verse. Indeed, Emerson is proclaimed the greatest man of letters of his age, destined to implant and protect an American culture, the interpreter of the Old World to the New and the New to the

Old, the censor of what shall pass, the jealous preparer of what is to come, the Moses, almost, of the modern migration. And, above all, the announcer of the Poet: "Unto us a man is born!" cried Emerson of Whitman. And he, in turn, is also recognized: "I met a seer, passing the hues and objects of the world," says Whitman.

"Rise, O days, from your fathomless deeps," Whitman commanded the new age, the age which should have been one of socially active idealism, revering anew the poetic spirit in man. But something went wrong; or, rather, the time was not ripe. All gross materialism needed purging away; instead, it continued to increase and proliferate until the American dream became a nightmare in which the rest of the world is entangled.

V *The Task Ahead*

Cresswell was left in a seeming dilemma. He had only recently announced that Whitman was, if not the first poet of the New World, at least the American Adam who numbered the beasts. Much more and many others could be expected to follow him in the coming of age of that New World. "The future for poetry and man lies in the guidance of that mysterious potent force, the personal Ideal, to its proper outlet in society, which so far only Whitman foreshadows, only America expects."[19]

But Emerson was neglected, and Whitman admired for only the wrong reasons and his weakest verse. Then, as the new century rolled on, it became increasingly more evident that all was lost, in America, in New Zealand, in the world. The poetic Ideal, the personal Ideal, was treated as the enemy of progress by all those involved in the Big Organization, mass man, mass production, mass materialism. It became clear to Cresswell that no poetry could flourish in the modern world until our scientific barbarism was shown to be based upon monstrous falsehoods and, like the choking weed it is, cleared from the soil of society.

Already, while working his way to England in 1928 as an engine-room greaser, Cresswell had had the opportunity to study machines at firsthand. Being ignorant of their parts, he was the more careful to understand them in principle—of which engineers and mechanics were mainly ignorant, he found. They knew no more of what brought engines about than of what shall bring them to an end. But Cresswell, holding that modern machines are evil, as their results show, determined to find in what their evil consists. How did modern machines differ from all mechanics before, as they must do, "considering that by their use Man is at length unable to recognize what was formerly held to be virtue, Providence, wisdom, prudence, health, necessity, and all settled order of Nature and supervision of Spirit before, but all things are now reversed."[20]

Cresswell became convinced that the original mischief of modern machines is explosion, or the burning of substances

in a way which provokes them to violence, by preventing their free dispersal. Which is to thwart natural disintegration when in process of becoming integration or harmony and oneness again, and is therefore to dabble in what is evil and devilish . . . . And this provoking to explosion, or hampering of natural combustion (if I use the right terms) being the opposite of oneness or harmony, is therefore that fatal and forbidden mischief we are warned of in all scriptures and oldest traditions, which men stumbled on in their reasons when Christendom fell. No former mechanics made use of this mischief . . . whereas these recent inventions that draw their vitality from explosion, being evil in themselves, may not be used except to Man's downfall. For being evil in themselves they can work only evil, *in their final results,* however palliative in their passing effects . . . [21]

That was written before ever the atomic bomb was thought feasible, let alone worldwide and almost commonplace. How time has sharpened Cresswell's argument! But in those days he carried those inquiries no further, although he was to come to them again.

Once more in England, he finished writing *The Poet's Progress* which, being admired by Arnold Bennett, was published soon after by Faber and Faber. This book was well received by the critics and, above all, by those perceptive patrons of the arts whose recognition was Cresswell's greatest reward. It was with those laurels freshly won that he returned to New Zealand, and was scorned and rejected. For by that time, in Cresswell's view, New Zealand had bartered her soul to the Devil, or to Technocracy, in return for apparent progress in the Great World; in place of her pioneering days' independence she was now set on the course that leads to bondage to alien powers. She had turned far from Nature and from the Poet.

Now in his thirties, Cresswell set himself to a new task, one never before asked of a poet. As each new era must rise above the debris of a past age, as modern science had destroyed the mythology of the ancient world, so Cresswell determined to destroy the mythology of the modern world, that is, its abstract science, in order to prepare the ground for a new age. This decision marked the end of the kind of poem he had been writing up to that time. That kind, even at its best, would serve his purpose no longer. We can see the bridge to his new style of work in the thirty-nine sonnets of *Lyttelton Harbour* in which he begins by scorning his native city for its rejection of the son who returned with honors hard won in England. He goes on to announce the present danger and dire future of his country, unless it heed his timely warning. And he ends by proclaiming his mission, divinely appointed to prepare the way for the return, after a time of tribulation, of the Gods and the rise of a new civilization on a newly scarified earth. He affirms his faith in Providence to this end, and his willingness to renounce all but a truthful following of his conscience.

Apart from an occasional verse and the delightful "pre-Chaucerian" *In Spring*, the sonnets of *Lyttelton Harbour* were the last poetry Cresswell was to write before his five or more years of prodigious labors in that Antipodean Hades—labors that were at length to sweep away the illusion of false science, to create a new Universe in which new men could live, and, in the end, free the poet to turn to his verse again. From that time on, Cresswell was to devote all his genius to a statement, in prose and in verse, in print or by speech, of one large view: that Man's faculties are now divided and at war with one another, and that they must be brought to harmony again through the instruction of Nature (which is matter brought to harmony by Spirit), which earthly harmony speaks to spirit in Man of his heavenly Parent. The orientation of all Cresswell's work in this one direction may explain some of the misunderstanding of his poetry and, in an age given over almost entirely to modern science and technology, the rejection of his prose argument.

VI   *Only Poets Shall Lead Them*

As regards political affairs, Cresswell held that *generally* a poet should be aloof or above active participation in political affairs, and so able the better to exhort or criticize or admonish those whose duty it is to direct affairs of state. He saw no salvation in politics alone, but only as the poetic or personal Ideal became alive and active in society, and thus able to inform the minds of the leaders and the will of the people alike. But he recognized that wise political action may ameliorate present distress and prepare for future renewal, just as unwise politics aggravates existing evils and stifles growth and renewal.

In *The Poet's Progress* Cresswell records how, as a young man in 1922, he was unable to resist involvement in the General Election campaign of that year in England, but rushed in on the side of Ramsay MacDonald in Wales where the battle was hottest. "It was the struggle as a whole that engrossed me: the noise and violence of angry and embittered voices, the lightnings of grievance and passion, and an outpouring of leaflets and papers that was like the litter of a colossal circus. . . ." But, at the moment of his victory, MacDonald's almost frenzy of elation, "like a man unprepared for greatness of any kind," destroyed Cresswell's faith in his hero. History was to prove his intuition true. That was the first, and the last, occasion on which Cresswell was active in political affairs.

But his keen and discerning interest in politics remained active all his life, in spite of his contention that no political creed could now save the modern world. In a dedicatory letter prefacing *Present Without Leave* he writes to his friend Ormond Wilson in New Zealand:

. . . it can do you no honour, as the youngest Member of our first New Zealand Labour Parliament, and a keen Socialist, to be associated with a work that so belittles our country and its prospects . . . . I don't believe the people in control here [in England in 1939] mean business; while your Party does. Here they mean business only when their safety's at stake. Now they're getting to work. But it's not for the poor and despairing, it's for themselves. It's to you I owe this comparison, and the new self-esteem it gives me to be a New Zealander, although I don't believe in your Socialism, your machines, science and Copernican universe in the least. But I see you are honest within that framework in which you believe; and while it endures I wish you well although it's my job to smash it to bits if I can.

We can best study Cresswell's gift for getting to the heart of social and political matters in his book *Margaret McMillan,* a memoir in which he paints a remarkably lively and sympathetic picture of the great social reformer and her times, interspersed with penetrating and enlightening criticism of governments and other institutions. Writing of the year 1865, when the young McMillan sisters returned to Scotland from a childhood sojourn in America, he notes that

in all cities, in all ages, there had always been poverty and overcrowding, but never hitherto of a kind and extent even faintly resembling this. Hitherto, in respect of the labouring population, their poverty had borne some relation to depression and scarcity in the nation at large; but now a new name needs to be found, and a new explanation, for a poverty and degradation which increased at precisely the same rate as the prosperity of the rest of the nation. It was the price the labouring classes were paying, not for the Industrial Revolution as such, *but for having lent their support to an insular and reactionary intervention abroad,* as Hazlitt alone of British historians makes plain; in return for which, at their bitter expense, their betters were now being rewarded in that worldly coin wherewith the Devil pays his own—a fabulous and exclusive wealth.[22]

It was hoped, by their "betters," that the great mass of the British people, with a Fleet to rule the seas and an Army to overawe the frontiers, would see the absurdity of wanting anything but ignorance, darkness, misery, and disease for themselves. England has lately repented somewhat, or been forced to repent, and has set to minding her own affairs; a lesson, Cresswell would add, to any country, his own included, whose intervention abroad cannot cover the evil in its society at home. That it, too, may be paid in the Devil's coin will not, in the end, save it from a yet more terrible and overwhelming disaster.

In writing of the meeting of the McMillan sisters with H. M. Hyndman, the foremost Socialist speaker and the English apostle of Karl Marx in the eighties, Cresswell notes that Hyndman, the son of a rich man,

was educated at public schools and at Oxford, and probably no other man of his class in England both held such enlightened views and preached them with such candour and vigour. He was quite untainted with the academic aloofness, the scrupulous moderation and tolerance which, while perhaps proper to pedants who teach, smack altogether too much of indifference in those who, having been taught, must next live and act in the World outside . . . . A total ignorance of learning and a knowledge of how the mass of the people live, though gravely inadequate, are a better equipment for governing a country than all this.[23]

Surely a most perceptive statement.

Cresswell then goes on to quote approvingly Margaret McMillan's effective criticism of certain churchmen's objections to Socialism, as a demonstration of both her power of generalization and *her* personal knowledge of the lives and needs of the great masses of the people and the causes of their suffering. And later in this biography there is a passage in which Cresswell admirably condenses his diagnosis of the cause of the ills of the modern world, and their only cure, a statement that informed his entire lifework, in prose and poetry. Let me here quote it in full. Commenting on the seeming cleavage between concern for the salvation of the soul and care of the suffering, afflicted body, he writes:

[There is a] deep cleavage between two seemingly opposite theories of perfection, a negative and a positive: that which has a want and deprivation in this World as its incentive, and that which has an abundance and fulfillment in the next world as its incentive. It is the tragedy of Christendom that these two opposite theories of perfection, which formerly were harmonised, have now been divided. The former is an idealised activity of the concrete or physical faculties, the latter an idealised activity of the abstract or spiritual faculties, and their harmony is necessary to a civilised human being. They have been parted and antagonised in modern times (that is, since the Reformation) by the insurrection of a third faculty, the reason; a mechanism which formerly, when subordinate, united them, but which now, when insurgent, divides them; and which, when thus insurgent and functioning independently of the concrete faculties of sense on the one hand and of the abstract faculty of spirit on the other hand, is incapable of apprehending the Ideal (which is their harmony) or anything but itself. In this depraved condition the insurgent reason is without restraint, and so proliferates itself profanely (that is, unideally) with each of the concrete and abstract faculties separately, as opposites, instead of together as harmony. With the concrete it proliferates itself as inventions and machines (an abuse of the concrete faculties which gradually degrades sense to be mere sensation) and with the abstract faculty it proliferates itself as abstract "truth" or mathematics (an abuse of the abstract which gradually degrades the Ideal to be merely knowledge and idea, i.e. pure physics).

Such is the modern scientific era which has risen on the ruins of Christendom and which, even since the recent discovery of the atom bomb, is still believed by its deluded enthusiasts to be the highest achievement of the human race. It is sufficiently remarkable that idealism . . . could persist at all in these circumstances. It did so by virtue of two other faculties, memory and desire, which are beyond the reach of reason, and so impervious to its insurrection, in all persons. In some persons (in whom memory predominates over desire) the Ideal, or memory of harmony, is preserved by these faculties; and thus preserved, it infects one or other of the divided concrete and abstract faculties, although it cannot, on account of the insurgent reason dividing them, infect both, or restore them to harmony. Neither the integrated human being of 400 B.C. (Greek Antiquity) nor of A.D. 1100 (Christendom) can, in this situation, recur—not until the division of Man's faculties has provoked those disorders between opposite and implacable ideologies whereby the entire rational system, and the merely rational, or Copernican, universe whereon it is founded, are overthrown. And although there are signs that this fearful corrective is not far off, until it has occurred, and the dreadful centuries of his regeneration have elapsed, there can be no harmony between the two theories of perfection . . . .[24]

So there we have it; the reader can now see that *this* poet has no soft words to soothe us. Cresswell observes that Margaret McMillan moved to Deptford at about that time, one of the poorest and most wretched of places in those years. Yet it was from Deptford that bold navigators sailed, in former times, to explore and exploit the rich unknown world, and to return with news and spoils, an excess of knowledge and wealth, to debauch and further divide Man's warring faculties. So much, says Cresswell, lay concealed in the mischievous notion that Man may safely and *publicly* investigate whatever he please. In the Church of Saint Nicholas at Deptford the poet Kit Marlowe lies buried. He foresaw in his Faustus the whole of this mighty human drama, the last act of which, Cresswell warns us, is soon to be played.

Poets are prophets, but we know how few unstop their ears

to them. Cresswell foresees our possible objection: if the foregoing
be true, of what avail for the future are the ideals and plans and
good works of such reformers as Margaret McMillan? To answer
our objection he speaks a parable, and then interprets it for us.

A hen turkey continued to sit immovable on its eggs in some grass
on the edge of sheep-yards, despite the sudden inrush of thousands
of sheep and numbers of yelling men and barking dogs, by which it
was soon hidden from sight. Then, in the midst of dust and uproar,
the turkey reappeared, perched on the yard-rail with an egg in its
beak, with which it flew over the neighbouring plantation. To the
amazement of those who beheld it, the bird continued to perform
this incredible feat until all its eggs had been carried to safety. [25]

Cresswell maintains that there must be in Man also, to a far higher
degree, an ingenuity to preserve his species in the midst of no
matter what worldwide disorders of overthrown reason, thanks to
something independent of the merely rational in his nature.
"Meanwhile, all that is done in love and care of the human species
... is a perfecting and preparing of that which will be found
inspiring and trustworthy still, when all else has failed."[26]

It is clear that Cresswell, unlike those others who turn their
backs on the modern world of science and super-organization, is
not trying to hark back to a nobler and simpler past but is an-
nouncing a new and civilized age, a new, and at first harsher,
earth—not even attempting to hide from us his belief that a
terrible clash of ideologies will intervene between now and that
time of renewal.

Let us now look at Cresswell's poetic progress, step by step, and
at his works in greater detail.

CHAPTER 2

The Warrior Awakened
and the Enemy Observed

I Early Autobiography: The Poet's Progress

IN 1930, when Cresswell was thirty-four years old, the first part
of his autobiography, *The Poet's Progress*, was published in
London. He records that he expected, indeed relied on, this book
to make a name for him in the literary world of England. But only,
he warned his readers, as supplementary, as a sort of pointer, to
his poetry which he insisted was all that mattered. "Poetry alone is
truth to me," he wrote.

His small book of verse that appeared in 1928 had gone almost
unnoticed, so that in a way *The Poet's Progress* was a first book;
and few first books live up to their author's expectations. But with
that publication Cresswell was by no means to be disappointed in
the impact it made—in the right quarters, too. Arnold Bennett had
read the manuscript, and had greatly admired it and introduced
Cresswell to the publishers. And when at last it came out Edward
Marsh read and admired it and wrote to Cresswell asking him to
lunch. The *Times Literary Supplement* reviewed the book, saying
that the author might yet prove a beacon to a bewildered generation. What with these notices and William Rothenstein's portrait
and kind sponsorship in the world of the arts, then, it seemed that
Cresswell's future was assured.

In literary circles in Cresswell's native land *The Poet's Progress*
has gained a reputation as "a gem of prose writing," "the unique
record of an eccentric character," and similar sayings. "He will be
remembered for his prose long after his poetry is forgotten," they
say. This last opinion especially annoyed Cresswell. Most of those
who still cherish the book choose to shut their eyes to its insistent

theme: the true nature of man and of poetry. In this they are like those people who cherish the Bible as literature while closing their ears to the hard sayings it contains.

The reader of *The Poet's Progress* must be ready to consider thoughtfully many hard sayings. He will get no further than the third page when he will read of Cresswell, in telling of his second departure from New Zealand, glorying in a fearful storm, with thunder and lightning, which accompanied his train past the Southern Alps to Christchurch.

For so I boldly believed, and thought it a good omen, that Heaven approved of what I did. Likewise I have had more omens since, and mostly from lightnings and violent storms, but sometimes from dreams, which things will scarce be believed in these crawling four-footed times. For so is this present age, the slowest and tamest that ever was. For if man were to move on wheels or on wings with the speed of light, to the soul he is thereby more clearly seen to be standing still. For time and place are in matter, and man is within time and place; so all that we reckon by time and place, to the spirit, hath neither motion nor life, as matter hath not. Know then, ye madmen and fools, the faster ye move and the more space ye explore, the more deeply ye are entombed in matter and time. Your fastest machines are no more than a funeral march, and the light of knowledge whereby ye are borne to the grave is the greeting of Hell. But fear not, but have faith. For God is love and courage and life everlasting, and so are ye. The ship that was to take me to England lay at Wellington, where I embarked, and sailed soon after. This was in April 1921.[1]

A surprising, almost a frightening statement; incredible in the progressive twenties. But time is telling. For what could then be smiled aside as youthful ranting, or even the small futile anger of a crank, now wears a more somber look. Savoring the cadences of this passage one is not surprised that, while modern ears were deaf to its warning, they were tickled by its style, mannered and archaic though they labeled it. But, as regards omens, they were not to be allowed to forget. For, many years later, Cresswell reminded them thus:

I think that not to believe in [omens] is absurd. For how else did the Ancients become what they were, and all for us, who now reap what they sowed. And pretending that these things were ill done, yet we live on their fruits . . . . The Consul Valerius was prevented from attacking the Aequi by a thunderstorm. And when bright weather instantly followed his withdrawal, he refused to renew the attack lest the Aequi were defended by some divine power. A modern general might have won the battle on the second assault, deeming such scruples to be nonsense. But how much more than a battle may the State have lost in the long run by want of piety? A wise man may prefer to lose what a fool can win easily. And Rome wasn't founded by fools.[2]

But the disbelieving could read on, forsaking faith in omens, to be enchanted by much else. Like this:

In the springtime the hills and woods round Cologne enticed me to take lonely walks, and now and then I would walk all night, or sleep out of doors. The forest roads were frequented by bands of youths and girls who sang to guitars and whistles as they went along, and these, and the wagoners with their loads of logs, turned my mind much to medieval history and to Grimm's *Fairy Tales*. In the forests east of the Rhine I saw the towers of castles I had read of in childhood and scarcely thought to behold again .... One night I bathed in a river near by, and made a bonfire, and slept in the forest. The city as well often put me in mind of that childish world, since in many places there are gargoyles, gables and carvings that belonged to a merrier time than this, and a harsher as well, being got by a closer acquaintance than ours, with life and death ....
I went once to Drachenfels, an occasion I never forget. It felt like a love-affair. I sat for hours on the summit, gazing down at the diminished river and the leagues of valleys and vineyards through which it flows. Except on such occasions as this, I learnt nothing by where I was, in this German town, since I lived in the past, or else in the future, and not in the present, of which I knew nothing; so time there slipped through my fingers like sand.[3]

II *The Kinds of Love*

Cresswell wrote some verse while he was in Germany. But at that time he was, as he tells us, still sunk in material things, writing from the fancied superiority and the natural wonders of his native land. Still, he was gaining experience, which he "had lacked so long." But now comes the first hint of that belief which he was to maintain as the basis of all art—the love of men for those of their own kind.

I took but a limited interest in women. To Poets, Conquerors and Kings it is the love and admiration of men alone that matters, and men have no such deep and lasting love for women as for heroes and poets, but only appear to in times when heroes and poets no longer exist. For love is like lightning, that for lack of a steeple will strike a tree. Women love men, men love heroes and poets, and these love the Gods; and this upward current is the cause of all glorious periods of faith and power on earth.[4]

There is of course, as Cresswell points out, a backward reflection of these beams, by which all creatures return the love of those who love them. So the highest *earthward* love of heroes and poets is towards not women but the men they lead, as these in turn requite the love of women; such being men's earthward love. "And therefore if it be thought that poets and heroes should love women before men, as though that alone were natural, then the same should be expected of men, that they should love, not women who love them, but animals, to whom women are next of kin."[5]

Cresswell observes that there are many exceptions to these general rules, which tend to throw doubt on them. Some exceptions happen because of metamorphosis of higher beings into forms that are lower. For example, the Gods, because they are Gods, can assume any form at will. And, similarly, a poet may, at times and for many reasons, become merely a man. And men may become like women or like animals, as is well known. Also, says Cresswell, the matter is further confused by the emergence of intermediate stages, which abound in present times: between men and poets and heroes, kinds which have lost the likeness of either; and between men and women, beings that share the nature of each, as is also well known. But Cresswell does not try to measure the depth of love or to order and confine its ways by rule or law. He wishes here to "show the cause of one thing only, why poets love men above women, why sometimes they do, according to the best of their nature; yet sometimes, I say, they do not, for the reason I now state, when through metamorphosis they are no longer poets but, for the time being, something less."

We shall hear more of this subject later, for Cresswell claims to demonstrate "the wholly masculine and homosexual origin and development of all culture." Another hard saying for times like these when not only do women seek prior right to those highest of affairs, the arts, but when men abdicate *their* right and responsibility, and turn to meddle with mere matter, and other unmanly pursuits. And that love which the Hebrew scriptures refer to as "more wonderful than the love of a woman,"[6] is degraded and so scorned.

If Cresswell now warns of the danger awaiting a poet who unwarily becomes for a time a very mortal man, then he writes from bitter personal experience. Although he nowhere mentions it explicitly in his autobiographical writings, there is a sonnet of that time, *To Freda Forsaken*, in which he maintains it is impossible to expect a woman to try to follow where he, the poet, needs must go; and bitterly be blames his own thoughtlessness for their tragic plight.

> Dear girl, I do not ask of thee that death
> Which to maintain thee daily were to me.
> Can the fish, needing water for its breath
> Exist on land and walk without the sea?
> Pure human maid, the low tide of my mind
> Had beached my weight and made us seem one kind.
> As in Romance, when fishes sue like men,
> I was awhile thy parching lover then . . . .[7]

III   *Eagle and Ant*

It was about that time too that Cresswell made the journey through Spain and Portugal from which travels, in midsummer heat and with little money, he returned to England in poor health and having written nothing of note while away. But all that time he was gaining experience and his poetic faculty was maturing. In a passage like the following we note a perception as keen as the eye of the eagle of which he writes.

Men have two eyes, one in the mind and one in the soul. Criticism is seated in the mind, and it is with this eye that [an artist] too often sees. But the eye of the soul is love, like an eagle's that sees all, and leads not away from life, but it feeds on all it can find. . . . It is only the nature that puts out all its roots in the dark in all directions, that loves that on which it feeds as its very self, even darkness withal, that achieves great things; and the meaning of this will never be told by any artist to the world, which could not endure to know it. Thus artists seem to be frank and egotistical when to themselves they are the most reserved of men, considering all they never say.... An eagle, which builds a most untidy nest, yet has whole countries under his eye, and almost the whole earth; but an ant has no range of vision like this, yet builds a most marvellous nest, and is sure and ingenious so far as it sees; which is not to compare the natures of the two creatures, but only as they appear. A great man, however, is different from each of these, being a combination of both, for while he sees like the eagle he builds like the ant, according to all that he sees. There is nothing to learn from the eagle that does nothing, but only from the ant. (Which were my chief companions in Spain, the ants, and the mountains, as I said.) To be born an eagle, and yet be instructed by ants: in this does greatness consist. But now our artists and poets and authors and men of science are like ants that were instructed by eagles, so they give up their true affairs and seek to inflate themselves and grow feathers. [8]

No wonder that, soon after this, Cresswell experienced that revelation while reading Keats, of which we heard before, after which all things were new to his eyes, and he delighted in all things, seeing them as children see them, for the first time as it were. Indeed, it was, he tells us, a return to that state of childhood he once knew, and the remembrance of natural scenes in Picton Sounds when those mighty powers spoke to him by day and night, although he was no more than twelve years old; which powers thereafter kept all his affairs in charge. Of the chief of those powers, his guardian angel, he wrote in a poem called *The Loss of my Companion Spirit*:

> He is not with me now for whom I wore
> Such happiness of spirit long before.
> To call him from the empty, shining air,
> Or from the same-shapen waves, what bliss it were! [9]

Cresswell now began to rewrite *The Ghosts of Foam*, and found himself writing an entirely new poem which he called *The Islands of Love*, but later he named it *Ode on the Triumph of Love through the Resurrection of Life*.[10] He wrote it in two days and never retouched it, considering it the first poem that was wholly his own. If we compare the opening and the closing lines of the two poems I think we shall see how much the poet has learned. *The Ghosts of Foam* begins:

By the shore at midnight lying
I hear the white surfs sighing,
"Bring them home, home, the brave who are born in dying,"
Bring each from his cold grave over the sea
Where no wild waves utter such anguish as we, . . .

Those, of course, are New Zealand's soldier dead who fell in overseas lands in the First World War. And in the middle part of this
poem are those optimistic lines we looked at before, lines about
building our perfect plains fed by unhindered healthy sun and
rains, not for any pageantries of death, and so on. And the poem
ends, somewhat grandly, with these lines:

Oh trees!
I believe in your beauty,
Though your falling leaves
Sing to me ever of the things that die,
There is your fluttering, imprisoned sky,
Not unreal,
Which the stripping winters cannot steal.
As in all, there is Paradise in you,
There is Paradise in you, and music rare,
In your boughs snared blue,
Like fancied isles of air,
Like flashing, far Hesperides
Summering in green, magician seas!

Green, magician seas! Yes, rather fanciful; but before that there
is just a hint of resurrection. Now turn to the *Ode on the Triumph
of Love* with its fresher language, strong and direct:

Thinking of war in the night
When the waves that arose on the shore
Were but sum and shadow of waves before,
New Zealand's soldiers arose to my sight.

Then where had been sea was an open pit
And what had been waves—oh Christ—were
ghosts surging out of it,
As they walked up from bottomless Hell
And ran at the last, and fell
At the touch of the sand,
And rose, and fled into the trees and over the land. . . .

And compare these concluding lines with those of the other:

> I watched the light sink
> From the hills to the sea's shadowed brink.
> But scarce was it there
> When from the forest burst, and over the shore,
> A sight more sudden and swift than the first.
> Happy, beautiful boys
> They were,
> Who ran to the sea without noise.
>
> As they passed
> No sound could I hear
> But a shout that gave speed to the last:
> "Come on! Come on! the sea's sunny and clear!"
>
> Soon their bodies bright
> Had brought to the welcoming waves their own
> breaking light.

Which is indeed a resurrection. From a long series of verses in which even the body of nature was buried in verbiage, something of spirit and life has arisen. But Cresswell was still far from satisfied.

IV   *Three Kinds of Men*

By now Cresswell was deeply unhappy again because of his private affairs, and because he feared the course he meant to take would cost him the love and respect of his family. He felt estranged from the rest of society, and saw only darkness before him. But if there were darkness, there was a dreadful joy too, because of what he held regarding the three kinds of men. There are in this world, he says, those who are artists, those whom we speak of as artistic, and those who are neither. The last of these kinds is the normal man, the highest of his kind being great statesmen and soldiers. Of the artistic kind, the best is the truly cultured man; but many are merely artificial. They are neither one with the natural man nor able to bear the pressure of suffering that the artist must bear. The world today, Cresswell maintains, has, apart from the normal man, mainly this merely artificial type.

But the artist is the man for whom abnormality and loneliness are the very breath of life. He has the power to transform pain into pleasure, not at will as with the merely artistic, but only when enough heat has been generated to boil or etherealize the matter of his suffering, which issues as great music, great poetry, and great art. And because he speaks from experience for and to the whole of mankind, the true greatness of his art is recognized, fame being an admission that an individual has returned to mankind from which, as an individual, his abnormalities had divorced him.

Cresswell recognizes the philosopher and the saint as also belonging to this kind of man. But the philosopher, when the pressure seizes and revolves his thoughts, relieves himself by logic and reason. The relentless power within the saint compels him to do noble acts. As with the artist, not will but necessity, by reason of the pain and mystery and darkness within them, generates heat and drives them to praise and to think and to do. "Saints," Cresswell remarks, "are mostly held to be greater than artists, more especially if their beliefs and actions led them to the stake. . . . Nevertheless they are no greater than artists, who burn at the stake throughout their whole lives, excepting the relief they have in the way I described."[11]

In those days, in the English summer and in the country, Cresswell tramped the roads and sold his poems, one for sixpence, to whoever would buy. In that way he made a precarious living and visited many places of historic interest, but with winter approaching, he had to return to London almost penniless. He knew that if he hawked his poems from door to door in that great city, he would be no different from any other peddler. So, to be honest with himself, he determined to throw in his lot with the street merchants and beggars. Remembering that Plato says, that a man may become rich from decreasing his needs as well as from increasing his wealth, he now gave up his shared room and his old manner of living as something beyond his means, sold all his personal possessions except one suit and the best of his few books, and went to the lowest class of lodging there is. One winter evening he and a friend of the streets who acted as guide to that strange and frightening underworld, stood in the line of shivering dispirited creatures awaiting admission to the Rat House. He who once had thought to live at ease by publishing the grandeur of his New World to the Old, now finally renounced those farfetched scenic effects and theatrical properties, tore up the paper world of two hemispheres, and began to found his life and his poetry on poverty and the hard path of lower-class experience. But it was a path brightened by unexpected friendships. Men even more desperately in need of help than himself often wished to guide him and to guard him from the dangers and pitfalls of their situation.

Men of this kind are often given to such little goodness; which in no way excuses their crimes; yet I must confess myself fonder of these small sparks of virtue in base natures than of all the justice and charity of those who make virtue a calling, whose property in goodness is unending. Perhaps because it is easier to know and to love what has limits. And surely it is more heartening to know that vice has its limits in all men than that virtue is unending in some; which last shows us only that evil may not be in some, whereas the former shows us that goodness must be in all. The one leads us to love and to follow some men, but the other compels us to love everyone, although we may not follow. And to love and to follow select persons belongs to religion and philosophy, which are yet subject to decay and to every abuse of abstractness, hollowness and hypocrisy, that promotes a reaction to a violent and unprincipled realism around it (as we see in these times). But to love all men and all things is poetic and the base of everything else. It is steadfast and incorruptible and always there to be found and built on when we need it, being Nature herself, or that compound of rare and gross, of abstract and concrete, whose harmony is the delight of poets. So that, when a too far-abstracted system decays, as with Christianity nowadays, not that opposite and utter materialism we see everywhere nowadays is the remedy, nor to mend what is past; but only poets have the remedy, by repairing our fallen parts, bringing those contrary and hateful opposites of our being together (as in Nature they are) when once the way is prepared for them.[12]

With the coming of summer, he again set out for country parts. The book he studied that summer was an anthology of modern verse, the reading of which strengthened his view that no poetry was then being written in England. While visiting friends at Bournemouth he renewed his study of music, taking great pleasure in listening to Beethoven. He sought to prove, in regard to music, the opinion he held in regard to poetry: "that Nature was at first a medium by which emotion was gotten expressed; but after, to the final confusion of art, this view was reversed, and Nature was now the chief matter expressed; and now, to her sensual kingdom, mankind was enslaved."[13]

Here he also referred to poetry, since the death of Byron, as the Sleeping Beauty imprisoned by Nature within impassable walls. He found that the same had happened with music: unlike Beethoven, to whom sound was the means and not matter expressed, later musicians made sound count for more and more until the art was no more than empty and sensual sound. Explaining further, he stated: "Once the medium of any art has begun to appeal, for its own sake, to the senses of men, the end of that art is in sight. For that is the greatest art which makes use of the senses only to appeal to the soul." The same, he asserted was true of painting, the very paint some artists used being held sacred, and texture and technique being admired for themselves alone. That winter he stayed at The Rat House once more, the last that he spent at that place.

V   *Descent into Hades*

During yet another summer Cresswell tramped the English countryside whence, as before when it pleased him to do so, he sent accounts of historical places to the New Zealand paper he often wrote for, the Christchurch *Press*. He was in London again when his first book of poems appeared at the beginning of 1928, receiving only a small notice in a corner of *The Times*. But Cresswell had already booked passage and sailed for New Zealand soon after, "that my pride might behold where at first I began," but "stricken with fear, as if now like Dante, I had thought of descending to Hell." And when, at the end of the voyage, they were nearing the Lyttelton Heads, "and saw the summits of the Southern Alps above a long bank of mist, arrayed in that ancient light which the Titans took from Jove, I looked with awe and delight on that dazzling chain of rocks, but my heart inquired, 'What country is this?' "[14]

In New Zealand he put all those things down on paper, as Part One of *The Poet's Progress*, the work that we have just been considering. This much was published in the *Press*. At the end of the same year he returned to England taking his work with him and, as we saw at the beginning of this chapter, it was eventually published in London and was greatly admired, bringing him a measure of that fame he so desired. For the occasion of that publication, Cresswell added three sonnets to his books, and he later complained ruefully that, while the rest of the book was often lauded, the sonnets were mostly unmentioned; and that this was a reversal of values in that it put prose before poetry, whereas all else in the book could only be justified by those three sonnets.

The first sonnet was written on the ship that was taking him back to England. It is a picture of the poet's resolution and triumph over the adversaries always awaiting those who challenge the wilderness of this world.

> Now I, in fear of going forth once more
> After seven homeless years so sore maintained,
> Take heart to hear how Dante was sustained
> By counsels made in Heav'n, which to him bore
> The upright shade of Virgil, leading forth
> His earthly peer from that full-evil wood
> Wherein the sharp-fanged she-wolf, Avarice, stood
> To stay him, and the lion, Lust and Wrath.
> Wherefore, I trust, whose mind is likewise bent
> On high and truthful aims, the upward way
> Through that same wilderness, for whom, as I,
> Those terrors lurk, like Dante will be lent
> The aid of Heav'n, since in this evil day
> He walks alone, and no example nigh.

Of the other two sonnets, both written soon after arriving in London, the first is perhaps the more successful, and by far the more moving poetic statement.

> Dear books! be all the nourishment I need!
> I am so poor I scarce have means to buy
> One meal a day. Alas! I must rely
> On your fair thoughts for all my winter feed.
> I famish for the faith and will to read,
> To find my spirit fit companions high:
> For that this world's inglorious I die,
> For no lean purse nor pauper's dish indeed.
> Be you my lamps; from every region shine
> Of that clear firmament whereto this age
> Stands but as stony earth, whilst you, afar
> From darkest night speak deathless things divine.
> Lean is his fare and bitter is his wage,
> On earth, whose nightly visitors you are.

It is indeed strange that only one or two reviewers noticed these sonnets. The others, evidently so blinded by the tinsel novelties of the age, or perhaps so dazzled by the excellence of the prose, failed to see these lines, in spite of awkwardness, as the true climax and complete message of Cresswell's book.

To consider again, for a moment, the earlier unnoticed collection of verse, *Poems 1921–1927*: Cresswell discarded most of the poems in that book and reprinted only what he considered the better ones, together with some new verse, in *Poems 1924–1931*. And of the poems in that collection he later in his *Progress* spoke lightly, pointing to them only as examples of the way he meant to travel to surer things. But the reader should not accept too literally Cresswell's own light estimate; he should investigate for himself, and he will surely find pleasure in verses that are Blake-like in simplicity—*The Poet's Heart*, for example:

> Plant thou in a poet's heart
> One dear word or look or deed,
> As the oak excels its seed
> So it will increase with art.
> On that dark and holy ground
> Didst thou drop one silent tear,
> In the season of the year
> Something mighty will be found.

And these opening lines from *Love and Reason*:

> Hell is unrest, and Heaven is true ease,
> Taught to the mind amid earth's quiet trees
> And meadows, where the sense hath deep delight
> From trees and flowers, the empty, trembling night,
> Or, through dim woods, from peepings of the sea,
> That, being bound, sets all its music free. . . .

Perhaps in *The Impatient Poet* we can best glimpse the clues to all of Cresswell's life:

> Love, men's honour, many ripening deeds,
> The level happiness of measured needs,
> From these the impatient poet turns aside

To see Apollo singing in his stride
From dawn till dusk. Once seen, how less it were
What men are kings, what women coil their hair.

All the time there lay at the back of Cresswell's mind thoughts
awakened by his study of modern verse. It seemed that he was being forced to a decision to do battle with the powers that were
threatening to utterly destroy poetry—even though, in the fray, his
own verse might suffer. For he would have to lay aside poetry
meantime and forge and take up that weapon he spoke of, a cool
and rational prose, and with it attack all in the modern world that
afflicts and imprisons the spirit of man, and all those little Canutes
that try to stem the tide-like return of civilization.

CHAPTER 3

The Labors of Hercules

I New Zealand Revisited

IN 1931 Cresswell returned from London to his native city of Christchurch. But he looked at this now strange country with eyes sharpened by his experience in England and an awakened poetic insight, and he made discoveries that, when he began to publish them weekly in the *Press*, proved rudely startling to his fellow countrymen. We have already looked at some of those writings, and even when they are not altogether condemnatory, it still is not difficult to imagine how deeply they were resented by a people wholly intolerant of criticism. In fact, the series of articles was abruptly ended, the contract annulled, and, with no money and no prospect of earning any in that place, a hurt and angry poet left his native city swearing never to set foot there again.

He made his way north to friends in Auckland. He had never lived in that city before, but immediately he felt freer in spirit and happier there, although at first he had few friends and none of his own age and tastes. He began to earn a precarious living by giving radio talks about poetry, ranging from the Ancient Greeks to some of the moderns. These talks were based on the essays he was now constantly writing and rewriting in order to further his projected Thesis on the nature of poetry and its dependence on the proper recognition of spirit in man—his "philosophy," he half-jokingly called it. Soon he discovered a little press in the heart of the city, run by sympathetic spirits, poor like himself, and there was published in 1934 a summary of several of his most recent talks. In this essay, *Modern Poetry and the Ideal*, Cresswell writes:

My aim has been to give you an idea of the downward direction of English poetry, and the loss of the personal and poetic Ideal in society, consequent on the rise of the scientific collectivist state. . . . We found the boy Tennyson carving the words BYRON IS DEAD on a tree, thus memorialising the end of a great race of English poets, the Romantic poets, whose lives and whose poetry were part of the French Revolution.

These poets, Shelley, Byron, Keats, and others showed the positive side of the Ideal, says Cresswell; the revolutionists expressed the negative side of the Ideal. The poets proclaimed that men have divine souls, and that society shall respect the personal man and his selfhood and provide or protect the conditions fostering his fullness of life. The revolutionists cried Why are we men debased, where is that light that once made us fully men? Let us out and find it, let us rebel. Politically they gained advantages, but they never regained the Ideal, the *harmony* of personal and social man. The poets showed men the Ideal, calling them to live again by its light, but in vain. Blake, for instance, "whose ears have heard the Holy Word that walk'd among ancient trees; calling the lapsed soul . . . to turn away no more. Why wilt thou turn away?" But by that time poets had become hopelessly separated from public life, and men didn't realize what was wrong with the world, any more than they do today.

They could think only in terms of political reforms, and ideas like equality and liberty—abstract liberty and abstract equality, that is. So they began to organize; for abstract ends and without the Ideal. That is where Science came in, promising man the whole world; and now Science began to take over the world and all mankind. Above all else Science can organize; especially can it organize in terms of abstract concepts, and in a big way. Indeed, it could organize a brand new abstract universe, not fit for natural man of course, but a mold into which it could force and imprison modern man. And after that the poets were not even thought of; nor their Ideal: the relation of man to nature, and man to society.

Tennyson, then, began the last phase in English poetry, the Victorian phase with its deserted gardens, a memory of lost Paradise, and its dry laurel leaves, its *physical* nature and its forsaken ladies—the Ideal forsaken by man.

But what is happening to *man* in poetry meanwhile, with nature looming so large; man who was the whole Ideal of nature expressed in poetry? Why, as nature increases in Tennyson so man decreases. The Ideal of man is being buried in nature, which is where the Ideal of man originally came from. Physical nature is covering him over, the Ideal man; which is exactly what was happening in the world of science out in the street. Soon there would be only physical man and physical nature left. . . . So man, in Tennyson's best poems, is always in a lonely forsaken situation . . . like *The Lady of Shalott*, who was shut in a tower and allowed to see who was passing only by looking into a mirror. Here she spends her time weaving a picture in tapestry of all she sees in the mirror. A perfect description, this, of the fate of the Ideal, shut away from the world, weaving its own shroud in the verses of the Victorian poets. [1]

All very delightful to modern science and the prophets of progress. Now, it seemed, poets could safely be let alone with nature, where they could do no harm. But poets won't be left alone or told what to do. Poets soon began to shock the Great Organization out of some of its complacent trust in the inevitability of progress. Cresswell shows that two poets in particular, first Walt Whitman in America and later D. H. Lawrence in England did this, often in verses that really were not poetry at all, but bold statements or declarations written in a manner that commanded the attention of the multitudes that had long forgotten what poetry was.

Whitman, at times, discovered the personal Ideal, as in those lines we read before, and in others where he speaks with authority, "as Adam early in the morning, walking forth from the bower refreshed with sleep"; or, "I am an acme of things accomplished, and I am encloser of things to be." But he was too often swept along on great tides of patriotism and glorious optimism. Lawrence was so estranged from society that he didn't quite rediscover the Ideal, didn't understand that man has any obligation to society, as society has to man. He listens only to the dark gods, as he calls them, within him. In their name he announces the personal self, or soul; which at least is a first curative step towards the Ideal. Lawrence himself puts it like this:

It is one of the terrible qualities of the reason that it has no life of its own, and unless continually kept nourished or modified by the naive life in man and woman, it becomes a purely parasitic and destructive thing. Make any human being a really rational being, and you have made him a parasitic and destructive force. Make any people mainly rational in their life, and their inner activity will be the activity of destruction. The more the populations of the world become only rational in their consciousness, the swifter they bring about their destruction pure and simple.... This is the tragedy of tragedies in all time, but particularly in our epoch: the killing off of the naive innocent life in all of us, by which alone we can continue to live, and the ugly triumph of the sophisticated greedy.[2]

A perfect description of today's Great Powers! Cresswell concludes his essay with the following words:

So the poetic Ideal, the human Ideal, throughout all these years since Byron, has come down to this, the dark personal gods of D. H. Lawrence. These are like the germ of the personal Ideal; but there's no hint of the social Ideal in Lawrence. The dark gods of Lawrence are only the other extreme of the Great Organisation he hated. The Great Organisation is the social Ideal grown malignant; the dark gods are the personal Ideal grown malignant, or gone native, if you prefer. Both manifest an utter division between personal and social man. The one is diseased for lack of the pure blood-stream of the personal Ideal; the other for lack of the essential outlet of the social Ideal. The future for poetry and man lies in the guidance of that mysterious potent force, the personal Ideal, to its proper outlet in society, which so far only Whitman foreshadows, only America expects.[3]

Truly that essay is the first evidence we have that the warrior is awakened. In the early poems, even those written after the poet had renounced the mere material view, there is no real hint of the battle soon to be joined. Even in *The Poet's Progress,* in spite of the radical views sometimes expressed, and in spite of all his condemnation of modern poetry, there is little to prepare one for the nature of the gigantic struggle ahead. Indeed, the poet more than once states his belief that taking up the fight against the false, at least in the field of philosophy, is no concern of his. But now, in this essay, the enemy has been sighted and named, Modern Science and the Great Organization, ruthless and brutal. The lady, the Ideal, must be rescued from the dark tower, which is of course the prison of the false universe.

But how shall this be done? Was not that expectation of America misplaced? In what does the power of the enemy consist? And how is it subtly used against man? And how shall the enemy be overcome? Cresswell, now faced with the mighty ramparts that prevented his poetic progress, was forced to tackle all those questions—alone, as we shall see. First, he had to write enough verse to justify his faith in himself and his task. This poetry now welled forth, raised perhaps in the first instance by those recent bitter rejections of his forthright stand.

II *Resettling His Native Land*

Still smarting because of that rejection by the city of his birth, Cresswell had written a number of sonnets on the voyage of *The Waterlily*, a ketch on which seven young men, friends of his, had rejected their country because of its inhospitality to their hopes, and had sailed for the tropic islands of the Pacific. Thus he thought their situation not unlike his own, and felt keenly their going and his loneliness. By that time, New Zealand had become two distinct countries to him: "on the one hand a social entity wherein I had no place, on the other a wild and half-supernatural ordination whereof I seemed to myself to be the only inhabitant."4 In a very real sense he had, by his writings, unsettled the country, conquered its innate nature, and settled it anew himself. Yet those few sonnets, published in *The Press*, were hardly remarked by the sleeping inhabitants.

Now settled and befriended in the North, and with the coming of spring, he wrote with fluent ease a poem which mightily encouraged him. It was prompted by his reading of some English verse of a period before Chaucer and of a simple and haunting concreteness. And yet, although he knew it to be a heron of a single flight, so fully had he come to terms with both the simple concreteness of such early verse and with the matter of his researches into the nature of the modern world, that he was able in this conceit composed in the archaic pastoral form to embrace all that his view of the modern world demanded in a sly attack. He called it *"In Spring"*. It speaks of a Summer the world may sometimes see. Here are some of its eleven verses:

> Winter now is done,
> And trees their show begin,
> They bringen out their flash
> Once more to make and spin.

> The birdies, while they work,
> Make music to their ears,
> To maken them more light
> The sweet sun comen nears.

Man and nature are in harmony:

> The shepherd by his lambs,
> And lovers two and two,
> They singen with delight
> To see them, what they do.

> You daffodils, you lamps
> That lighten Summer near,
> You need no longer shine
> For now that she is here.

And then on to our cold dead world:

> But minds of little men,
> Like engines of irôn,
> They maken no new leaves
> Nor beds to rest upon.

> 'Tis Winter in the world,
> Fly all who comen thence,
> The hollow cave is here,
> The ivy curtain dense.

But the poet brings us hope, and shows us the way to the Fair:

> But heartis love is green,
> Come shepherds here to play,
> And live and love with me,
> I tellen you we may.

> Winter now is done,
> And trees no longer bare.
> The leavès comen forth
> Like people to a Fair.[5]

Such are the sweet joys a poet earns to lighten his way. And, at
that time, Cresswell the poet enjoyed a time of some happiness,

but for Cresswell the man, Winter was to shroud most of his life.

About that time, too, he saw that much more could be made of the verses he had written on *The Waterlily*. Working in this direction he enlarged the scope of that theme, and soon he had produced a poem of thirty-nine sonnets which was published by that same little press founded by Lowry and Holloway, the Unicorn Press. He now added an Introductory Note, and called the whole thing *Lyttelton Harbour*. Critics were immediately aware of a power and poetic authority greater than in any of Cresswell's earlier and shorter poems.

The occasion and the clue to the meaning of this sequence of sonnets were, as we have seen, the voyage of the seven young men of Cresswell's old school in the ketch *Waterlily* for some years among the islands of the South Pacific. Their aim: to return to Nature, perhaps to paint and write, generally to live like natives of that region. But, after nearly a year of adventuring, the ketch was wrecked. The crew, minus all their possessions, escaped in the dinghy and were saved. By devious routes, and after various trials, they all eventually returned to their homeland.

In his Introductory Note Cresswell points a moral: that Nature, while she welcomes and rewards all those who flee from the mean and repressive conditions of modern life, will nevertheless not be a patron and protectress to men, *save to Mankind as a whole*. It may be interesting to note that in another context, that of Christian philosophy or doctrine, which always has honored and encouraged the recluse or the hermit, Pope Paul VI now writes of the Christian concept of a new world in the Encyclical Letter, *Populorum Progressio*, that there can be no progress toward the complete development of man, no real civilization nor true culture, without the *simultaneous development of Mankind as a whole*. The foregoing is another example of those sharp insights which Cresswell often tucks away in little notes or dedications, almost casually, yet which constantly surprise and delight us.

The poem begins with the poet rejoicing in the harbor's rocky pools and experiencing a kinship with Ocean's children, the tiny denizens of the pools; and, homeless and disowned by his own kind, he feels like the exiled *Waterlily* crew.

> . . . Even as they I leave
> A thankless city and a flatter'd race.

Homeless, yet having all, like them I cleave
To thy fierce skirts, O Fortune! and I trace
My life in thine, O Nature! and believe
To be alone thy child is no disgrace.

Then, as a messenger of Nature, commanded since childhood to
proclaim her sovereignty, he sorrowfully warns his countrymen,
"scholars in the modern school of sheep," what they must do.

Whose heart is not with Nature, him the voice
Of the vain World and pass-word of the hour
Misleads. But with one gift, the patient choice
Of truth, doth she her silent few endower,
Asks in the heart what's answered in the flower,
In the wild storm and raging waters' noise.
Such, to those few, are as the steps of power:
He to his fastness climbs who these employs.
Yet he is fain to turn towards his kind,
As I to you, far London, erst did come,
And found you wanting! tho' your practic'd mind
Approved my aims and, honour'd, sent me home.
And proudly I return'd, only to find
A further, darker Thule than ever yours to Rome!

He meditates on the strange beauty of the rock pools, and his
poetic intention is strengthened as he considers how such beauty
came to be.

'Tis not the moon that with her naked light
Doth leave these world-wide copies of her skill,
These carven rocks, bare sands, and treasures bright.
But in the waves how doth her pencil still
Her task perform! Even as my spirit will,
With thy near aid, O Nature, come to write
What 'tis her heavenly office to fulfil;
Else were she ever muffled in all night. . . .

In the next eight or nine sonnets he speaks of the time he stood,
"a fond ambitious child," before his country's constant hills and
abiding streams, full of promise and greatly protected by Nature
for his devotion to her, until these later days when he was ban-
ished by a boorish and misunderstanding race. Only the trees,

the laurels, and his old school's fields, "where he might not excel,"
soften his anger now.

> A spirit to thine arbour draweth near,
> A child whose angel soul is still its shame;
> Fond waif, the foundling of a Hemisphere,
> Now steals among you as before he came,
> And parts the curtains of thine only fame
> And marks within the dazzling meadow clear
> Of thine immortal mid-day, and the game,
> And there the well-knit striplings of the year.
> Well hath he known thy path; and well within
> The light and shade; and one bright Form beside,
> A God whose love they thoughtless strove to win,
> That whisper'd, and the thicket parted wide,
> 'Go, tell the World thy vision and *its* sin!'
> And pluck'd some leaves, and round these temples tied.

His vision and the World's sin! There we hear the poet beginning urgently to proclaim his henceforth constant message and
warning: that Nature is our only Mother, nurse and teacher, being
not merely matter to be subjected to men's desires nor material
ot be exploited, but the ever-present harmony of Spirit enlivening
the physical forms of Nature. And the sin? Men today ignore the
poet's message to their dire peril. They exploit Nature for selfish
gain; worse, they exploit the evil that is inherent in matter when
Spirit is not only ignored but denied; as once in Eden man, in
rebellion against Spirit, ate the fruit of forbidden knowledge.
And that at the urging of the woman Eve.

Here, too, in his poem Cresswell emphasizes his belief that
modern woman, rebelling against her allotted part in creation, and
envious of man's ascendency, is replaying the role of Eve by
tempting man with a vanity of knowledge to pander to material
desires and a deadening luxury; and that man should learn how
properly to honor man and manly knowledge instead. "But foul
their sin if men their spirits sell to woman, . . . whose price of
worship is the sickly smell of incense offer'd to the golden calf,"
he says.

Men, in his own country as in the rest of the world, plunder
and destroy too the native inhabitants of the newer lands they
invade, and reduce to mockery the Church and her Founder.

They are not arm'd that have their quarrel just
Whom you disarm with kindness and deceit,
And in the God you trade in bring to trust,
To plunder where they worship at His feet.
The Cross a gallows and the Church a cheat
You make, that sav'd you when the Caesars' lust
Had made the World one city, and one street
Toward it, and your little lives its dust.
That Church He left you when the Saviour rose,
That temple of His spirit, ye unbuild,
Till the green Earth whence all believing grows
With false attempts and foolish ruin's fill'd.
Man's memory dries. The summer of these woes
Once more must spring from Earth, as only Nature willed.

But, cries the poet-prophet, justice is at hand! He likens Christendom to the young men's sailing ship, voyaging through perilous seas to a new promised land. Her captain's knowledge is betrayed, and the vessel is wrecked. Now there is only the storm-tossed ocean, and no open port.

And from the shore I mark its fever'd crew,
The Powers of Man (but millions here in one)
A famous band. And sad it were to view
Their voyage end, who think them but begun.
Yet is that Christian passage all but done,
In greed or stupor sunk. And ye that blew
Them here, O Nature, is there landing none
On this far shore for shallow aims untrue?
Long calms delude; but on the deep I spy
Hell's pitchy whirlwind racing to the spot;
While from the bowers flute-throated voices cry
'Midnight remembers morning's songs forgot!'
Alas, I dream! Man's doom and ruin nigh,
These things I know. But any hope is not.

No hope? No, cries the poet, confessing his error; there is one only hope for man:

Lately I have seen . . .
The olden Gods from furthest Hades swarm
To these Antipodes of where they last
Left Man to die, who in the impending storm
Launch'd that brave vessel with the Cross its mast.

The last three sonnets of the sequence announce the poet's mission, his protection and providence in Nature, and his complete
dedication to the course his conscience keeps.

> For thus am I, a spirit sent before,
> But one of many whom ye would not hear;
> To chance too us'd, and to the World's uproar,
> Embracing doubt once that black storm was clear,
> To faith unfaithful with no Hell to fear.
> Awake! and know this wild familiar shore,
> And that worse hell that from the deep draws near.
> No other land there is nor rescue more.
> Round its bright peaks the raging void in vain
> Shall beat its surge; when here the God returns
> To tangled groves; when Phoebus here again
> O'er all its vales for Hyacinthus burns
> With cloudless light, delicious to the swain
> Hard by the dashèd ales of many mountain urns.

> Ye barren hearts and bitter, steep'd in brine;
> Ye empty lives where nothing native grows
> In that bare world ye worship! Here in mine
> Proudly within her covert climbs the rose,
> Where in the dark the horrid satyr goes
> To dabble in the brook that feeds the vine,
> And hide him when the morning-breeze half-shows
> The watching Pleiades within the pine.
> Then Phoebus' coming the complexion'd cloud
> Shall turn to silver; and the merry Pan
> Awake the Muses in their mountain shroud;
> And all the sensual growths to music fan;
> And on the rock the cricket cry aloud
> Like morning singing in the heart of Man.

> Enough! no more! the World is round me now
> With its lewd eyes, and hath been many a day;
> And happy if these tokens on my brow
> It turn to shameful thorns, and to repay
> My love with loathing. Nor I cannot stay
> With thee, presageful Memory; but I vow
> My spirit to thee, tho' each step away
> The rough years drive me onward. For I know
> One light like thee before me as behind,

> Immortal beauty in its morning fair,
> Unearthly in its evening of the mind,
> And in its noon a heat like this I bear
> Within me now. He only is not blind
> Whose conscience keeps one course, nor needs he
>   to despair.

Nothing quite like *Lyttelton Harbour* had appeared in New Zealand before. Its full import probably escaped most readers at the time of its publication in 1936, and is only appearing now to a younger generation who read it in the light of contemporary events. Some critics quibbled over what they called Cresswell's use of archaic language; but it will probably trouble the new generation no more than the use of similar language by Shakespeare or Milton or Blake, for the reason pointed out by Allen Curnow, a poet younger than Cresswell, who declared that "in the best of the sonnets these ["archaisms"] become a living speech."[6] And as such they will outlive changing fashions.

In any case, these sonnets represent a climax in the poet's development, and they contain the key to all that followed. Some critics hold that they are Cresswell's most successful work. That, however, is a simplification that disregards too much the complex issues of the last twenty years of the poet's life.

III   *Vulcan's Forge*

Now, having established a maturity in poetic outlook and a certain mastery of verse, and having announced himself and to what purpose dedicated, Cresswell could turn to seeking out the inner lair of the Enemy. In what did his secret power over Man consist? By what means could he be most effectively destroyed? The poet's further progress seemed impossible until this was done. He sought for an entry, to launch an attack, but could find none in any view of poetry he had hitherto expressed. Any new and deeper view of poetry, on the other hand, seemed somehow to embrace the whole universe and lay beyond his grasp. Without knowing it, he wos preparing for that attack on the Copernican Universe, in the name of poetry, that he was soon to attempt.

In the difficulty I was in I went to my books, and began reading the Ancients, who always move me the most from being nearest to con-

crete nature; not nearer than Chaucer or Wordsworth or Ruskin, or
many moderns; but nearer in their public system (which is how
poetry appears to me) than any society since. In this way I hit on a
fine opening, on which I could build a whole thesis, as I thought;
and I continued to add to this with great pains, but without knowing
where I was going. . . . And although I nearly finished what I thought
would suffice, I soon began something else; for being once embarked
on philosophizing I couldn't keep the matter under control. This second business which began with Emerson and Whitman, came to look
like a history of America; while yet a third thesis, that began with
Blake, was soon at sea with the British fleet blockading Napoleon.
. . . However, I knew that with time I should write my thesis; but how
long a time? And how large a matter must it be in the end! . . . and
yet it led me in the end to the greatest discoveries, from which all is
to come, if I can be worthy of them. It was only for this I was sent
back to New Zealand, I see. [7]

It was in Auckland during the next four or five years that he
fashioned his formidable *Thesis on the Mechanism of Spirit or
Poetic Intention in Man,* laboring unceasingly, if not untiringly,
to perfect it, often sitting at his table for five or six hours over
some difficulty, almost without writing a word. In Part Two of
his *Progress* Cresswell gives many moving descriptions of his
labors to master the matter of that Thesis. Here are a few. [8]

I took a lodging nearer to the centre of Auckland, overlooking the
harbour. Here I began work on the third Thesis, which was larger
and more intricate than the other two, although it by no means made
plain those feelings and certainties about poetry and the poetic future
of Mankind which now more than ever were haunting my thoughts,
setting me, I was certain, apart from all other men, and placing a great
weight upon me when, as it seemed, I was least able to bear it. . . .
I was more and more in my labours becoming convinced that what
afflicted this World and must overthrow it was a deep and *organized*
cleavage between concrete and abstract in our faculties, whose harmony was poetic and the labour of poets, and the only refuge before
Mankind. . . . What was at stake, I know now, was the harmony of the
poetic with the rational faculties (concrete with abstract, as I said)
which modern science has so deeply divided, and which modern art
professes to ignore. . . .
Each attempt I now made seemed at last the conclusive one, until I
was halted by some difficulty, when my recent clear writings would
become patched and tangled with amendments from which at length

a new line of inquiry would emerge. I often put it aside from exhaustion and the want of any impulse to go on. . . . I gave a good deal of time to drinking and carousing with new companions I was finding in the hotels and bars in town. I never felt so strong an impulse to this distraction as now, nor ever yielded to it so recklessly. Either this was because all my faculties, high and low, were aroused to their greatest activity by my researches, or else because I was more than ever sensitive to the vulgar and virile attractions of my surroundings in a country wherein these things have more validity than its culture, or because my mind was so lonely in this work, and under so great a strain, that a reaction to a seeming looseness of principle and low company was only a natural and healthy relief. I think the last reason most likely, and allowing for the other two. For the results have been sound, and have fulfilled all my hopes; and nothing of strength and excellence ever came out of what was weak and vicious. Moreover, when this work was done . . . these excesses diminished of themselves without any effort or discountenance on my part, until in the end it was as natural to do without them and to look to a new plane of experience as before to do so had been almost death. . . .

But whether I was in funds or not, at any time that my Thesis was going well (I should now almost call it my philosophy!) or whenever some difficulty that stood in the way of its being concluded had been overcome, I was so triumphant and so confident of doing something of great importance to the World, that my little hut and its half-boarded window, its worm-eaten table and mass of covered and corrected and so old and dirtied manuscripts (and in the midst of them the last, the divine one! that now was true and perfect and led me to clean sheets and clear writing, like to new pastures, once more) these things were of more glory and gain, I thought, than a kingdom, even than all the kingdoms of Napoleon and Alexander the Great put together. But when it went badly, I felt as if I were dying.

Such, and so arduous, was the toil of these Auckland years; in summer he sweltered under a tin roof, in winter he was often without enough blankets and fuel to keep warm. Now and then he got a little money in return for radio talks on poetry; and, where it was washed up on the beach at Castor Bay, after being jettisoned from overseas ships, he sometimes found enough vegetable food for a meal when his funds were low. With the completion of his Thesis, Cresswell, who had declared war on the Enemy in *Lyttelton Harbour,* had now forged a weapon against him, strong but sharp and pliant, not for himself alone but ready for use by all those who might be called to serve after him in the same warfare.

But now, before considering the fate of the Thesis, let us take a look at some interesting observations in the earlier versions, parts of which in typescript are in this writer's hands. Cresswell begins one passage by noting that "a prosperous people, long indulged in tranquility, looks to the state as its providence, and no longer to nature." As a result, nature no longer speaks to personal man, or to social man, of the harmony of the spiritual and the physical, which harmony alone leads to true taste, integrity, and every other virtue of a people or nation. In place of taste there is indulgence, by many mistaken for freedom. By not distinguishing evil from good, such indulgence by degrees extinguishes the good.

A poet born into such circumstances must either long lie dormant through antipathy, or flourish too early, through the warm incentive of relaxed opinion and the little depth of his roots in nature. In the first instance he withdraws from society, to receive his identity from nature alone; in the second instance he is too early attracted from the influence of nature to that of society. In this second event he exhibits a fatal maturity very different in effect from the precosity of too abundant genius, of a Milton, a Keats, or a Shelley. These last in their infancy strangle serpents; in their prime they subdue Cerberus and plunder the Hesperides. But our modern poets, springing up without roots, forced beyond their strength by the heated relaxing air they imbibe, do like Gods for a little, and thereafter like modern men. . . . They might do better; but their growth, being drawn out so rapidly, quite outruns their experience.[9]

Any renewal must slowly rise from the soil again. Signs of such a renewal will be seen in the use of language:

The poetic use of a language appears to involve a gradual increase of rhythmic intensity, a quickening of pulse, until the utmost metrical potency is reached. Thereafter, as in the furious metrical follies of Swinburne, any further progress is like whipping a dead horse. In this situation it were better, as in Tennyson, to lighten the load, to deal in more flimsy matter . . . less pressing to the moral and political intellect. . . . When content is thus subordinated to metrical form, when the load is lightened that the measure may live, when personal man, in his present and living environment is forsaken by poetry, then poetry has little further to go. But in its beginning, its infancy, as I believe will be found in the earliest literature of every people, we hear the slow irregular pace of that beat which maturity shall quicken and intensify as expression and content fall more and more into step, of a poetic power shouldering, yet still immobilised by, its greatest load: the divine meaning of nature to personal man and his meaning to society. We hear the heart-beats of the half-animate mass, the advent of a people, of an epoch. Without intensity, poetry, pulse and form cannot be.

Cresswell listened for that faint heart-beat in the newer lands. In the uncouth speech of the backblocks was there not evidence that even spoliation and avarice paused now and then, inhaled the fresh new air, and saluted nature? "Let us look to America!" he cried.

History will find that the four greatest men of the first American century were Washington, Emerson, Lincoln and Whitman; a soldier, a statesman, and two men of letters. Emerson, it appears, was destined to implant and protect an American culture, to renew the intellect, as nature had already renewed the environment, of mankind. With what assurance, with what certitude he stands by the sea between the Old World and the New, the interpreter of the one to the other, the censor of what shall pass, the jealous preparer of what is to come: the Moses, almost, of the modern migration! . . . He calls on the elements, on health, supremacy, power, as the fields call on the sunlight, the downpour and the lightning in spring, that their barrenness be redressed. . . . I have no intention of directly comparing the rustic Muse of Emerson with the very mature and profoundly derivative Muse of Tennyson. Indeed, I do mean a comparison; but subject to this understanding: the last days of a superb and transcendent literature are sure to be lit with an autumn glory, a reflection and blaze from the summer and solstice of the race; yet the sowing and promise of a subsequent spring and its first lowly and vigorous shoots do merit a devotion and care out of proportion to the ease and surfeit with which we gather the fruits of the fall. Be it known then, my ear in the matter is neither faulty nor misinformed; but it begs leave, knowing well what it does, to adhere to a different taste from that wherein the last hundred years of English criticism have instructed us. It is not all for music nor satiety. It welcomes the rustic furrow of Emerson's verse. It delights in the few first green shoots of Whitman, though these are yet without indolent fruits, and so few of so many that fell on stony ground. It prefers these Spring trials to an autumn prolonged now to the pitch of rottenness. . . .

Any spiritual refreshment which may have befallen man from this vast migration from one half of the Globe to the other has at first sight been more than cancelled by a terrible, perhaps a disastrous, increase in universal materialism. But poetry stands in a peculiar and exclusive relationship to current events. The genius of one man is enough to save her light to mankind; while the despairing immolation of millions avails nothing to defend a weak or impious civilisation from certain ruin. We look on materialism, therefore, with one mind, on poetry with another. We deplore mechanical, soulless, shifty, over-weening, callous America; but we welcome Whitman. In proportion as we detest the one we shall welcome the other. . . .

Events move on. That sowing (from man's new and hazardous contact with nature) accomplished, they may yet, indeed they must yet, visit the world with suffering and disaster, as the Corybantic thunder and lightning and tempest deluge and deafen the greening fields. But terrible as the material sequel may be to man, disastrous as it must be to those flying fugitive straws of the former prime, the green living blade is not beaten down nor dismayed. It hears the thunder with joy, it looks on the lightning with love, it bows to the deluge with delight. There is in every renascence of poetry a certain future for the soul of man whatever temporal course events take. . . . Poets are the interpreters and epitomes of the Divine ideal manifested in nature to man. Through its poets a people perceives and assimilates this ideal, which a poet sees written in one language in nature and translates in another language to men. The fullest association with nature and the impact of events, their transmission through poets and their expression in language, become fainter through time and dis-tance from those events, at length resulting to a people in a weakness in respect both of its poetry and its character which may not be re-paired otherwise than by a new contact with nature and a new con-flict with events. In which new situation a people must once more not be lacking in interpreters of that contact, with ears able to hear the Divine message to man whereof nature is ever articulate. . . .

Destiny appears to have seated modern man on her throne, and dis-tracted him with the barren empire of knowledge and science, in order to effect her own vital purpose unobserved and disguised, when even his solicitude had been more fatal to the new life she intended than the bite of an adder. In some countries they burn fires at night near the orchards lest an unseasonable frost destroy the fruit. Such is the splendour of the approaching end of our system, to be a world-wide curtain of fire about the still unripe field of a new poetry and a new being to man.

In the version of his Thesis which deals, in part, with the poet Blake and the French Revolution and the rise of Napoleon, Cresswell has something to say regarding a purely intellectual enlightenment, such as that which attempted to help the fallen masses of Europe in the eighteenth century. The weakness, as much as the strength, of this effort, and the need of a new ideal of personal man, gave rise to the French revolution and the advent of Napoleon, whose fateful career was a natural response to the passionate longing of men, and a merited chastisement of a purely intellectual enlightenment.

In man the intellect tends to become more and more a social and collective function, however that function be selfishly misapplied, deriving its exercise from the dependence of men on each other, and seeming to flourish even in the absence of the Ideal; while that in man which we call the personality remains a profound and baffling enigma, to all but the boundless solicitude and inscrutable insight of nature. The intellect, therefore, is never a cure of those social evils which have their origin in the loss of the Ideal and the consequent disease of natural and personal man. If the derivation of the Ideal in nature be disallowed or disturbed, that is to say, if nature be secularised, then the intellect itself, however active, astute and magnanimous, is diseased; a fact which our educationalists and reformers appear not to notice. The application of an intellectual relief to a natural disorder is an aggravation thereof which calls alone for the vengeance of the loftiest personal genius. Such was the terrible antithesis embodied in Napoleon. Such were the extremes of pedantry and despotism between which the Romantic poets were outcast from mankind. . . .

We see therefore that modern mechanical science, so absurdly called progress, in supplanting the ideal conception of nature and man by a wholly physical conception thereof, in bringing man more and more into utter dependence on that gross and inferior conception through the media of machines, in thereby annihilating the natural ideal at its source, and with the ideal the prestige and meaning of personal man in relation, on the one hand to society, and on the other hand to his Creator, is bent on the downfall and destruction of organised mankind. . . .

IV   *The Sharp Sword*

These first essays certainly cleared much ground of the tangled and rubbishy growths of recent decades; they affirmed certain fundamental standards, and pointed the way to an honest advance. But they by no means satisfied Cresswell. So much, he foresaw, might be said to be only opinion, or not based on unshakable principles, or in some other way able to be turned aside. Although it might surprise, hurt, and even bruise the adversary, it perhaps would not cut, cripple, or slay. Some sharper weapon was needed. Thus, when Cresswell had at length polished the final version of his Thesis it proved to be a very different piece of writing: nothing less than a cool and fully reasoned, but most concise, argument proceeding step by step from first principles to consider the creation and nature of man, of his providence in Nature, and of the issue of these matters in poetry and art, of man's several civilized systems and the reasons for their fall, of his condition today and of his hope to come.

What became of it? For reasons we may touch on later when, too, we shall look further into that remarkable work, the whole thing was turned down by Cresswell's publishers. In a manner typical of him, after the first brief shock of rejection he tossed the thing aside and plunged into poetry again. This time it was to be his blank verse drama *The Forest*. His labors in philosophy were over; for a time his astonished Enemy had fled in disorder, if not from the whole world at least from Cresswell's environs. The poet's field of action was cleared; his mind was refreshed and at ease, but zestful for *poetic* triumphs. So great was that personal victory—the reestablishment of a sane universe and a fertile earth, the clearing of the way for poetry to follow—that it scarcely mattered that the rest of mankind continued to grope blindly in ignorance—but it seemed a pity an artist or two did not open their eyes.

If the world was not, at that time, destined to see the results of Cresswell's years of lonely labor, it did have a shorter version of the Thesis brought to its unbelieving notice. That was *Eena Deena Dynamo or the Downfall of Modern Science* in which, in a more racy manner (the manner of his radio talks) Cresswell restated the more important of his findings, though without the full and closely reasoned proofs. That essay was published in 1936 by the Caxton Press of Christchurch and it consisted of thirteen sections.

In "I: Showing to whom this speech is addressed, and who make a fit audience," Cresswell says: "I must warn you that nobody can properly talk to both sexes at once, as they pretend to do in our Universities and public meetings." Although, of course, there are some grounds common to both sexes (much religious ground and some ground of law, and marriage and its various concerns), he contends, the higher and more characteristic faculties of each sex, and certainly the innate understanding, cannot be addressed in both sexes at once. And he points to the peak of greatness in the civilization of Ancient Greece to provide an example of the proper relationship of the sexes in an orderly society, noting that what he calls the homosexual tradition of culture left a profound and lasting influence of Greek life—a lesson, he maintains, that our age must learn before it has any pretensions to be thought civilized or cultured.

This is a broader and more far-reaching view of the statement we read in *The Poet's Progress* regarding love between men and women, and between men and poets or heroes. Both views are equally distasteful to the modern world, so that, in some quarters, Cresswell has been scorned as "an advocate of perversion" and in others as a woman hater. Would he relegate all women to a position of absolute inferiority?

As regards the first charge, Cresswell in his writings, as we shall see, makes it clear that he is speaking of a relationship as far removed from the perversions of the modern world as the sun from subterranean darkness. As regards the second charge, it is interesting to note that on practically every occasion where Cresswell has recorded his praise and respect for a person, and acknowledged his indebtedness for wisdom and understanding, that person has been a woman. Only a few years after *Eena Deena Dynamo*, Cresswell wrote in *Present Without Leave* of his friendship with Lady Ottoline Morrell and emphasized that this lady had sharpened his perception of personality more than anyone had ever done:

... in her love of truth and honesty she gave up nothing that was naturally feminine, nor anything that was gorgeous and liberal in her birth and upbringing; but she joined a richness of feeling and all outward faculties to a deep insight and zest for all things of the mind; and seeking all things that were most praiseworthy and admirable, yet she remained fully herself and her sex. In this way she much raised my estimation of all women (notwithstanding there remained many differences of opinion between us) by so lessening and making light of that gap between their higher natures and ours, of which I had always made most; although this discovery, as in the case of others of my new friends, only came with time.

And a few years later still, in *Margaret McMillan*, Cresswell wrote a memoir of a woman in which admiration is almost unbounded. In letters to friends, too, he warned them not to take too literally some of his earlier views. It is therefore less the stark pronouncements than the truth behind them that we should consider: that in only the few most spirited men are the powers of creation and leadership truly realized, and that, perceiving this, honest men will forsake wives and home and comfort and follow such creative powers to death if need be; and that, in contrast, the modern world, by every exploitation and titillation of sex and all manner of pandering to luxury, has brought womanhood to a state lower than ever before in history. And if we can go thus far with Cresswell, may we not then exclaim with him how idle and worthless are those present activities we call modern education and modern culture!

In order to show what *is* culture and education, Cresswell asks us to consider how the modern world differs from former times. He holds that the difference lies in a new relation, or rather unrelation, of the reason and the senses which has led man to a new system of so-called knowledge about Nature—that is, the Earth and its furnishings about and beneath us, the Universe beyond, and a network of inventions arising from this so-called knowledge. Our senses, as we know, provide us with *concrete* knowledge of objects and their properties; with our reason we related things and so have ideas. But our reason, being stirred from within and being able to work apart from contact with concrete objects, provides us with what we call *abstract* knowledge. It is the former healthy relation between sense and reason, or concrete and abstract, that has been disturbed in the modern world.

Cresswell is sure that we will agree with him that man cannot be at peace with himself nor with Nature, nor able to create a civilized society, unless his senses, his reason, and all his faculties *are* in perfect relation or harmony. "In the earlier World," says Cresswell, "Man, by this harmony of all his faculties, that is, of his reason with his senses, and thereby his harmony with Nature around him, evolved the utmost safety and happiness which by

his spirit, or instinct of harmony, he was able." It is this instinct
that expresses itself in a people's culture and in the education
of each new generation.

Man, as far back as we see him in history, is begun in this task of
culture and education by some instinct within him which leads him
to spring up and dance, strike drums, chant music, draw pictures,
speak poems, or however express some dimly-felt rhythmic relation
between parts of things seen, or things heard, or things felt, some
instinct within him that all things which his senses perceive are in
harmony, and purport or signify a superior oneness or being whole. . . .
The cycle of the seasons, the movements of the heavenly bodies, the
rising and setting of the sun and moon . . . these awaken an answer in
Man on account of the same law or harmony being implanted in Man
as in all creations of Nature whatever. Moving the limbs, or making
sounds, rhythmically, or representing objects and actions harmoniously
in a picture or a poem, or pursuing ideas harmoniously as in reason,
these actions are merely expressing an instinct Man has that parts of
time, or parts of sound, or concrete parts of Nature, and necessarily
all Man's dealings therewith and ideas thereof, are harmoniously related, and so signify some mysterious unity which Man in this way
tries to express, whenever its influence posesses him. This unity can
only be Spirit or God, and the many divinities Spirit assumes as parts,
which Man feels as an influence within him and tries in this way
to express.[10]

It is in this way only, Cresswell insists, that any system of faith,
and of social harmony such as morals and law, comes to be and
makes it possible for Man to grow. To this ideal of the harmonious and the beautiful all else is subject. And this is Man's
culture; his state of being civilized. In any race, all studies adapted
to this end, and no other studies, are education. We see, says
Cresswell, that savages have more in common with civilized
peoples than we have, since we are neither cultured nor civilized
—that is, using all our faculties in harmony, one with the other
and with surrounding Nature.

Cresswell then asks us to look at the only two former civilized
systems produced by the European peoples: Classical Paganism
and Gothic Christendom, both of which are quite alike in their
harmonious relation with Nature, and in the harmony of Man's
senses and reason which necessarily accompanies that relation
with Nature. And in all they did and founded, in their systems of

morals and law and in their social organization and their public religious observances, in their prime there was that complete harmony between their higher and lower faculties, between the concrete and abstract.

Nevertheless, there was one important and, as one system followed the other, an essential difference between them. In the first system, that of Classical Greece, the senses or concrete faculty became the originating or active extreme; in Gothic Christendom, it was the reason or abstract faculty. Although these, when thus described, seem opposite systems, and in the way stated are opposite, they are indeed identical or complementary in that in both systems the senses and reason were in harmony, and Man had the same view of Nature in each. No matter how a few thinkers might *privately* indulge in abstract speculation, Man's reason might never *publicly* contradict his senses, and so threaten the harmony between them.

As Paganism, in its decay, gave rise quite naturally to Christendom, we should expect Christendom, in its decay, to give rise to a new system of Paganism. And so, says Cresswell, it must. But as several centuries of turmoil and darkness occurred between the downfall of the Ancient World and the full flowering of medieval Christendom, so we must be prepared for such centuries of disorder, essential to such a great change, before the rise of a new order. Indeed, the disorder may be even more terrible because a more drastic change is necessary; nothing less than an entirely new view of the Universe.

As we saw, the senses were the active faculty in Paganism, the impulse to harmony being from sense to reason. During the decay of any civilization it is the active faculty, its mission done, but still predominant, that becomes the impulse toward disorder; this we well know from the downfall of Paganism when the senses were unhinged and credulity, cruelty, and sensuality ran riot, and the most preposterous follies and license flourished publicly. Now we live in times that, since the glorious flowering of the Renaissance, carry us deeper into the decline of Christendom. And, if we are not blinded by the malady of our times, we see that it is now the reason, in Christendom the active impulse, that has become the impulse toward disorder, as in the nature of these changes we should expect. Now the reason has become licentious and extravagant, unguided by its opposite faculty, the sense; and reason must pass to its downfall and abasement before a new civilization can arise, whose impulsive extreme must needs be the concrete or physical sense once more.

Cresswell then draws our attention to a most startling way in which Christendom in decline differs from Paganism in decline. When formerly the decadent senses were the impulse toward disorder they still did not change Man's conception of the Universe because the senses operate only from Nature to Man, never from Man to Nature. No matter how degraded they become, the senses leave Nature as they find her. Consequently, upon the rise of Christendom, with reason the predominant faculty producing a renewed harmony with the now disciplined senses, the new age quite naturally accepted the Ptolemaic Universe of the ancients and indeed the same view of all Nature.

But, as all things come to over-ripeness and their fall, so did impulsive reason, after the marvelous ripeness of the Renaissance, move to its fall. Reason, greatly conscious that it can work entirely from within, entirely abstractly as we say, and now disdaining the discipline and guidance of the senses, became presumptuous and shattered the former harmony of Man's faculties. As Cresswell puts it:

. . . reason straightway announces new and startling discoveries in Nature, notwithstanding that nothing is true in fact, however it be seemingly true in theory, that isn't in harmony with the senses. And thus reason by degrees comes to fabricate that disordered and licentious conception of Nature which is the modern or Copernican Universe. Which modern Universe is disordered and licentious . . . because the reason that conceives it is disordered and licentious (through acting alone and without regard to harmony with Man's other faculties).[11]

But have not the discoveries of modern science given us a whole new world of wealth, inventions and gadgets and technology enough to enrich all our lives? All these are indeed the fruit of the tree of our "new knowledge." Do not look too closely, though, for evidence of the blight. For every seeming benefit there is a more disastrous consequence. Apart, even, from the horrors of scientific warfare and increasing internal violence, we are all obliged to lead more and more unnatural and unhealthy lives, leaving the future to ponder how to cure our **fearful** mental and organic diseases; leaving the future to educate everyone to live by idealism while today provides the means for unscrupulous nobodies to lead selfish and indolent lives; leaving the future to cope with a mounting pollution of every element of our environment.

But modern science cares nothing for moral considerations, but only for what reason *thinks* to be truth. It has divorced itself from that relation with virtue and harmony which was the glory of ancient science . . . since only by that means could it *progress*, as it likes to describe its proceedings. And here the gulf between discord and harmony can be summed up in a sentence. The dissolute and licentious reason asserts that only what is 'true' is wholesome and beneficent to Man; the poetic and harmonised faculties of Man assert that only what is wholesome and beneficent to Man is true. There is literally a World of difference, a World of downfall and disaster and suffering to come, between these two standpoints.[12]

Cresswell now asks us to consider the question: who then shall heal us? His answer is, of course, poets and artists, because they are the kind of beings inspired by the outward and concrete. They are thus gifted to lead Man again to a true use of his senses, to come to his senses, we could say, after his nightmare of reason has become wandering and licentious—just as, on the downfall of the Ancient World, the kind of beings inspired from within, or abstractly, led Man by reason and a chastening of his then licentious senses to wholeness or harmony. And these, we know, were inspired teachers and prophets, and above all they were inspired by Jesus Christ in whom all extremes were perfectly harmonized and made whole.

Today, teachers and reformers try by reasoning to correct Man's disordered faculties but cannot because the senses, neglected in our merely rational Universe, have sunk from true sense to be the evil and degenerate aspect of sense, or sensation and sensationalism; in that form they are quite out of reach of reason, and thus wholly ungovernable.

In this form they share more and more in the modern World, not in the view nor control of reason, but as the participators, patrons and passengers of its inventions and machines. The senses can't participate in the use of inventions and machines, since they don't participate in their conception, which is effected by reason alone. But the senses when divided from reason, when sunk to be only sensation, not only participate but revel in machines; and it's this blind and degenerate faculty which is increasing all over the World every minute. . . . And this is the faculty, degenerate sense, or sensation, which our teachers and educationalists are vainly trying to bring under the guidance of reason; while each new invention, like the wireless, and birth-control, and upholstered flights through the air at greater and greater speed, and the cinema, and the vast sex-advertisement ramp of our beaches and streets and shop-windows and books and newspapers, all these and everything else only feed and increase the growth of sensation at a more and more uncontrollable rate. . . . No one man will [overthrow dissolute reason and annul its results]; but dire and fearful events will do so, wherein Man shall have nowhere to turn for comfort and guidance but to certain gifted beings called poets; not those little mannequins of the fashions, whether political, intellectual, or sensational fashions, who are called poets now, but beings through whom and by whom the divine meaning of Nature shall again appear to Mankind, beings in whom Man's faculties will once more be seen in harmony.[13]

But, says Cresswell, in times like ours, when poets stand alone and must do battle with the World single-handed, they should be critics of all things as well as artists, taking care to arm themselves by snatching from their mighty opponents the same weapon those enemies lack the skill to wield with precision themselves; that is, a cool and highly rational prose. "This now is what poets must wield, taking care not to turn this sharp piercing weapon against themselves but only against those enemies of Mankind who misuse it . . ."

By which Cresswell means that the poet should never confuse his two valid modes of expression, but ever keep his poetry free of intellectualism and his prose clear of pseudo-poetic obscurity. One sure way to turn the "sharp piercing weapon" against himself is for a poet to aim his verse almost solely at man's rational faculty, loading his verse with abstract concepts instead of concrete images. The opposite, and equally dangerous to the poet-critic, is an addiction to a prose style lacking in precision by attempting to carry the argument on concepts that are pseudo-poetic, the result offending against logic, the very faculty he should strive to delight. We may see this confusion in the language of, say, a Chardin compared with a Maritain. Let there be the least confusion between the role of the poetic and the rational faculties, says Cresswell, and the enemy triumphs, because in the one case he can expose the verse as weak and futile and turn the attempted intellectual thrust against its author, and in the other case he can treat the prose as a smoke screen and find cover in it to pursue his own wicked aims.

Let there be no doubt about it, any lack of clarity in the criticism only masks the real nature of modern inventions and technology which, Cresswell asserts, arises from the craving of the isolated reason, now divorced from healthy association with the senses, to propagate or embody itself in matter which it now seeks as its true opposite. Reason, seeking to know and embrace matter as fact, finds itself baffled and can contemplate only itself, or reason again; as the outpourings of many scientists often show us. But what now degenerate sense can and does grasp is matter as sensation; and the effects of these unmutual meetings of our divided faculties are inventions or machines, which are reason embodied in matter but insensible, and equally matter motivated by reason but irrational, and in all essence divided. This is the basis of Cresswell's further assertion that the evil of machines is not due to their abuse; it is inherent in their nature and infects their every use. Mankind is being taken for a ride!

Narcissus, wandering afar from his divinely appointed domains, gazed at his image in a certain pool and became enamored of it (not of himself, as some would have it) thinking it the nymph of that place. Utterly unable to attain his desire and inattentive to the sensible ministrations of the mountain nymph, divine Echo, who would have healed his wandering desires, even with half-remembered words, had he listened, he was shocked and numbed by his despairing situation and at last killed himself. His name, Narcissus, is from the same root as narcosis—numbness, drugged irresponsibility. This is a picture of modern man, numbed, drugged into irresponsibility by the fixity of his enamored gaze into the mirror-world of science, mistaking for reality this figment of his own reason while its technologies both feed his fascination and increase his irresponsibility until he threatens to destroy himself.

CHAPTER 4

The Gods Speak

I *New Zealand Critics*

CRESSWELL'S views, as a whole, found little support from fellow New Zealand poets and other writers; though most of these were radically dissatisfied with modern society and often proposed ways to reform it. But chiefly each criticized only that aspect of society that seemed to him most faulty. The majority largely accepted the scientific or intellectually rationalist view of the modern world, and sought reforms only by means of new political systems, or new educational theories, or a greater encouragement of cultural activities (but those "cultural" activities, from Cresswell's point of view, could only proliferate the seeds of artistic decadence). One or two did see the urgency to end the exploitation of Nature and begin cooperating with her age-old laws; chiefly by means of a reappraisal of the practice of agriculture, and by a new respect for the country's natural resources. But those few were never heeded by the politicians and received little encouragement from the general populace.

This is not to say that there are no significant echoes of a similar cry in the voices of Cresswell and his contemporaries in New Zealand. During the years Cresswell spent in Auckland there was a small but active company of writers and artists, R. A. K. Mason, A. R. D. Fairburn, Frank Sargeson, Vernon Brown, Lindsay Fraser, Jane Mander and others who found in each other lively and congenial fellowship. They used to gather at Lowry and Holloway's press or at Blake's coffee shop in nearby Vulcan Lane; while just over the road was the upper room of the Queen's Ferry pub for later sessions and less intellectual company. Cresswell, however much he

relaxed toward these fellow artists socially and enjoyed the give
and take of conversation, remained aloof and often silent regarding
his poetic aims. Yet one has only to read the works of his contemporaries to become aware of a general climate of pessimism toward
the future of New Zealand, and the world, and occasionally a note
of prophecy not unlike that of Cresswell.

The short stories of Frank Sargeson show the inimical influences
at work in New Zealand society (his later novels portray these influences growing in grotesque and horrifying menace), balanced
by the rejection by his waifs of the generally accepted conformist
roles and aims of "progress," and a kind of salving in "mateship."
But with Sargeson the downfall of the forms and structure of our
system, its scientism and technology, is implied where Cresswell
makes it explicit. Sargeson shows us the evil sheltered and fomented
by puritanism affecting and stunting the lives of men and women
and provides a view of curative graces; but he doesn't delve as
Cresswell does into the philosophical causes and roots of the evil—
if the modern pursuit of matter leads to evils, then when did that
forbidden curiosity arise? And why? And in what does its enchant-
ment consist, since modern man, like Marlowe's Faustus, can no
longer enjoy the spoils of his sorry bargain?

R. A. K. Mason is in some ways strangely much nearer to Cresswell than are most of the other poets then writing in New Zealand
—nearer in intensity of the knowledge of evil overshadowing good.
Mason's verse is often Spanish-like in the terrible contrast between
its blazing white light and black shadow—like the etchings of Goya.
In many ways his poetic outlook is much more personal and quite
unlike Cresswell's; but in these lines from *Sonnet of Brotherhood*
we recognize a Cresswellian image:

> ... then what
> of these beleaguered victims this our race
> betrayed alike by Fate's gigantic plot
> here in this far-pitched perilous hostile place
> this solitary hard-assaulted spot
> fixed at the friendless outer edge of space.

A. R. D. Fairburn, breathing a milder air, at times rejoicing in
a mellower sun, often sings of the joys of the native scene and the
satisfactions of rough but loving toil on the land. But listen to Fairburn too:

... The earth
is barren, the stream is dry; the sun has blackened
grass that was green and springing, flowers that
were fair.

Those lines are from his long poem *Dominion* which ends as follows:

... stars burning through the worldwide air of chaos,
hissing in icy seas, black winds
shaking space, the shrieking
darkness pierced by flames
from the cracked shell of earth ...
... black earth, stillness of ash. ...
In the beginning was the Word:
and in the beginning again shall be the Word:
the seed shall spring in the blackened earth
and the Word be made flesh.

Which is Cresswell's vision, Cresswell's message too.

In New Zealand's South Island two other poets writing at that same time also echo Cresswellian themes. They are Charles Brasch and Allen Curnow. Curnow's verse, more coolly intellectual than that of the Auckland poets, owes nothing to Cresswell, but here again is the prevailing note of pessimism. This, for example, from *Not in Narrow Seas*:

Enemies have crossed the seas
And hold the passes that enfold you upward. ...
Come these to sing your agonies, not upward,
Where the two islands not in narrow seas
Shrink in a wind from the world's nether ice.

And this from his poems of the same period, *Enemies*:

No more burns the fire within the word.
... Great waters
are come upon the world, all cold
untroubled by birth and death alike.

Charles Brasch writes *In These Islands*,

> . . . meeting and parting
> Shake us, making tremulous the salt-rimmed air;
> Divided and perplexed the sea is waiting,
> Birds and fishes visit us and disappear. . . .
> And none knows where he will lie down at night.

However, in *The Silent Land,* after stating that "the mountains are empty . . . the plains are nameless and the cities cry for meaning," he also writes:

> So relenting, earth will tame her tamer
> . . . Ah then
> For him the Oreads will haunt the fields near
>   the snowline,
> He will walk with his shadow across the bleaching plain
> No longer solitary, and hear the sea talking
> Dark in the rocks, O and the angel will visit,
> Signing life's air with indefinable mark.

Nature becoming man's earthly Mother again and the heavenly Father peopling the mountains and plains and seas with his divinities once more and then cities ringing with song—so Cresswell too foretells. Although Cresswell neither influenced nor was influenced by his contemporaries in New Zealand, we cannot fail to see the sympathetic climate in which they met and regarded one another. It was mainly Cresswell's unique philosophical writings and the manner in which these at times affected his poetry that his fellows found disconcerting. In brief, although they were sympathetic to most of Cresswell's aims, they considered his publicly expressed views preposterous and ridiculous at times, and his continued advocacy of them either obstinate naïveté or futile arrogance, or both. University circles appeared to sense a danger to their institutions and, while politely patronizing the man as a rare eccentric, developed a self-protective coldness toward his works. After all, it was only what was to be expected and Cresswell paid no heed either to their indifference or to their criticism.

II THE FOREST *and Another Departure*

During the remainder of his time at Castor Bay, Cresswell worked on his blank verse play *The Forest*. But his eyes were already turned toward England for he was sure that, having completed the *Thesis,* the task that had driven him to the Southern Hades was done. While he welcomed and enjoyed the refreshment brought by contact with Nature in the New World and with men reinvigorated by life in outback places, he well knew that the Enemy was already taking over and debasing them. Soon he would be looked at askance as idle and alien. In England, on the other hand, he still hoped to find encouragement and publication amid the last remnants of an old civilization, the last ramparts of cultural integrity, fast failing though they were. "It wasn't so much a matter of having to go to England to write as having to go to England to live," he told the *N. Z. Listener* (February 10, 1950) on his last visit to New Zealand. "When I came back here once I was left on the beach. An axe was put in my hand and I was told to go into the scrub and cut trees! If I've got to die in poverty I'd rather do it in London than on the steps of Parliament Buildings in Wellington." Having armed and equipped himself in the nether Hades of New Zealand he determined to set sail and work at poetry alone, in England.

When at last he took ship at the port of Wellington late in 1938 he carried with him a first draft of *The Forest,* plans for a verse drama based on the life of Napoleon, and on the voyage he completed the second part of his *Progress* trusting that it would reopen doors that the first part had opened to him once before. But Hitler, seen by Cresswell as the first of poetry's ghastly avengers, was now in Munich and, although the book was published by Cassell in 1939, the outbreak of World War II overshadowed its reception and threw all his plans into chaos, even to the extent of his shelving all work on the nearly completed play. Truly, the sonnet he placed at the end of *Present Without Leave* shows that such an interruption to a writer's plans is to be taken with patience and humility.

> Not men know the purpose compelling their actions,
>   however they argue.
> Only the strong-will'd Fates, and the terrible Furies
>   their agents,
> Balance all things in their scales and even all
>   things hereafter;
> Only these know the design of the work and what lies
>   before us.
> Darkly we labour, as men live in dreams when asleep
>   in the night-time,

Deeming they wake and they do this and that, but 'tis
   shadowy Morpheus
Fashions our dreams; on his errands we run, as we find
   in the morning.
So do we toil, but awake, and for masters far stronger
   than Morpheus,
Knowing that ours is the work, not knowing the plan
   is another's.
Ah, but if men were not blind how the little they'd
   see would mislead them!

As with the sonnets in *The Poet's Progress*, this poem seems to
have passed the critics' blind eyes. If only they had read it aloud,
how that ominously insistent beat might have warned them to open
wide their eyes! *Present Without Leave* also contains lines from
two poems that Cresswell wrote in the flush of his excitement after
laying aside the Thesis: "Invocation to Apollo" and "Hymn to Hy-
perion". In these Cresswell attempted to translate into the medium
of poetry the theme of his researches: the approaching end of the
era of false science and the coming again of the pagan gods whom
he addresses by their Greek patronyms, not because he saw any
sort of classical Greek revival, but because, as he said, he knew no
other names. No doubt, although Cresswell attempted a concrete
expression of his theme, these verses suffer because of that classical
Greek flavor and, if noticed at all, were regarded as merely exercis-
es in the classical style, of no moment to moderns. It may be said
that, had Cresswell shared the Maori traditions of some of his
countrymen, he could have invoked the gods under their Maori
names. And when they come again, who can say what their names
may be? But listen to these lines showing how, under Christ, Man
was less a natural inhabitant of this Earth by having in all things
to choose between two supernatural extremes, Heaven or Hell.

Wherefore to choose
Between two ways of disinheritance
By equal loss of earthly nature: one,
By attraction of that pure unearthly light,
The perfect Christ, th' aerial sentry; the other,
By vassalage to that encroaching dark,
Devouring Chaos, who from matter robs
Th' access of heavenly light.[1]

The passage goes on to show how Man, now having forsaken the evidence of his senses and trusting in the seeming truth of scientific instruments and appliances, is finally ensnared by

> The enticing snare of him who aims,
> By auxiliary increase of feeble sense,
> To enfeeble sense the more (as when the limb,
> Relying on a crutch, wastes quite away)
> Until his dark dominion be complete,
> And Man, the outpost of divinity
> In Nature, to the disastrous Fiend deserts.

But, says Cresswell, in the Southern Hemisphere Nature is expectant of its new deities. And he predicts final victory over the Enemy:

> She for thy certain coming keeps a path
> Nor god nor spirit nor migrating Man
> Hath hither trod, but thine inaugural foot
> Foreshadows to the World.

III   *The Untrodden Path*

During the war years Cresswell was engaged by various Government departments to lecture to the troops, chiefly on the subject of New Zealand. This work entailed some traveling, and left little time for writing poetry. But after the war he took up *The Forest* again, a comedy in three acts, and it seems he completed it near the end of 1947. But it was 1952 before it was published in Auckland by the Pelorus Press.[2]

The Forest is certainly Cresswell's most successful and most sustained attempt to portray concretely his view of the modern World. It deals with the divorce between Heaven and Earth that has given Lucifer, the fallen Archangel, control of the World; concurrently, it deals with the divorce between man and woman that is both cause and symptom of the disharmony of Man and Nature. And the story that carries these themes to a triumphant outcome is a very typical New Zealand situation: the proposed sale to a lumber merchant of a large tract of forest-clad mountain country for the felling of the timber thereon. In just such ways, first by the pioneer settlers to clear the land for grazing, and later

by timber milling merchants, most of the hill country of New
Zealand has been denuded of all native forest, and indeed of all
tree cover, and is now subject to slips and to every form of erosion, the cause of destructive floods. It was of this despoiling of
the country that Cresswell wrote: "Thus that mirror of Nature
was cracked, the most flawless and heavenly the eyes of men ever
beheld on earth. The great bulk of men are monsters, whom freedom makes drunken, whom profit alone attracts."

In the play, Mr. Salter, a city tycoon who has made his pile,
puts a large part of his money into a great tract of mountain
forest, magnificently grand and remote, builds a house in this
retreat, and plans to retire there and seek peace of mind and soul
—an almost alien yearning aroused, he scarcely knows why, by
the sight of Nature's encircling grandeur. In this he is encouraged
by his son Clive who has as friend the young poet George. It is
to Clive that Salter exclaims:

How lovely is the forest in this light!
Most ancient state of Nature, more you seem
Than lovely to the sight, a spirit rather,
A presence and a power that makes it strange
How you should fall, so many million years
Dissolving in a moment's smoke that Man
May find new ways to prosper. Now I see
This World's a feint, and human happiness
A monstrous shadow . . .
In times like these, in Nature's perfect hours,
Our spirits rouse us to another World
And lead us thither, leaving far behind
Our cares and all our comforts. In this hour
Our wondering senses wake to know themselves
The highway to our hopes. Ah, Nature then
Is not herself, but this eventful Earth
Is but a step in some ascending stair
Whose end's in Heaven. To be her butcher then
Seems the most evil, and a murder done
To my own spirit. . . .

But, when Salter is ruined by Lucifer to further his devilish
plans, Mrs. Salter urges her husband to sell the forest. She has
little use for a house in the mountain wilds, but she needs more
money for her city society rounds and for spending on her only

son, Clive, for what she fondly imagines to be his good. Clive, though, is something of a disappointment to his mother. He has no eyes for the wealthy city girls, wishing only to share the companionship of George in wild and country places. Such friendship, he asserts, is more natural to young men than pandering to the romantic wishes of spoilt young women, and more productive of poetry and all the arts. Obviously, thinks Mrs. Salter, he is very much under the unhealthy influence of that George who calls himself a poet. She urges him to marry.

Not yet, says Clive, but later perhaps,

> ... if I find some young woman
> Who's plain and homely, and never heard of love—
> Your kind of love—who can cook and keep a house
> And rear ten children, maybe I'll take her on.

And when his mother asks him, if women mean so little to him, to tell her what means more, he replies, "Call it Nature."

"What's Nature, then?" Mrs. Salter asks.

> *Clive:* Oh, I don't know. (a pause) She's seated in
>   our hearts,
> Not in our minds. She's what men truly are,
> Their very souls. Within us she is love,
> Outside of us she's all that's beautiful.
> But look around you!
> This is her seat, her citadel, herself!
> Drive her from here, the oceans and the air
> And all the starry archipelagoes
> She's mistress of, where she's impregnable.
> This World was once her University
> Where those degrees with honours might be got
> Whereby men graduate to an after life.
> Creation is the school she's mistress of,
> And she's as great in little as in much
> And wise in all things. Deep within our hearts
> She is desire, and older than men's conscience.
> When outwardly we fall from her control
> She must be sought within, and far beyond
> Our worthless reasons. She chooses whom she will

> To hear her voice and tell it to the rest,
> Who, if they will not listen, their disease
> Grows fatal to them. This Age is one of those
> That's never heard her voice, and when it does
> Will die of it, and not know what it was
> That struck so terribly.

Mrs. Salter, now convinced that Clive's friendship with George is doing him no good, realizes she has both son and husband against her. She confides in Bishop, the unscrupulous timber merchant, and urges him to force the deal, free her husband from the spell of the forest, and make it possible for her to acquire the money she so much desires. The forest, of course, is a symbol for much else in danger in our times: all that is beneficent and natural which an acquisitive society tends to destroy quite ruthlessly. Not only our hills become bare and eroded skeletons, and our rivers either beds of dry stone or silt-choked torrents, but our towns and cities become strident, neurotic, and destructive instead of being the gracious civilized communities that cities should be. Our lives become dry and hard and eroded—like the hills when the forest is gone.

Because hers is the sex thought most to desire pampered luxury and artifice, modern woman is apt to be portrayed by Cresswell as a temptress. He shows us Mrs. Salter, a twentieth-century Eve in a New Zealand garden of Eden, tempting her husband against his own newly found better judgment. But the apple is a bitter one. And, in the end, Salter sends Bishop packing, and refuses to sell his forest; he has been listening to the poet George.

> *George:* . . . when the mind
> That's native to the heart shall come to rise
> Above this sadness and to shoot its rays
> Over that ground of sense which we desire,
> Until the sight of what and where we are
> Is clear as mid-day, we shall know the road
> We travel to our graves without regret.
> . . . Our hearts are where our senses stand
> To dote upon this Earth, as you do here.
> And the affection felt, and hunger for it,
> This is whereby men rise, and is the base
> Of all they build. Our reasons are the sun

That travels round, which if we do forget
This Earth it shines on just to dote on that,
It strikes us blind, till like this present World
We fall, and find our senses with the ground . . .

Thus reason, in itself, is only worth
As brittle glass, a window to the heart
That's like a room our senses beautify
To make us rich in reading all we own.

IV *Bargain with the Enemy*

Such, in brief, is the story on the natural level; but above and beyond these earthly dealings there are all kinds of goings-on on the supernatural level. The play begins with a long conversation between the archangel Gabriel and Lucifer regarding a "peace" treaty resolving Lucifer's rebellion, that has been operating for a long time now, but which seems in danger of breaking down. Gabriel has been sent from Heaven to Earth to investigate and report if the Devil is playing false by tampering with his side of the bargain. When the Devil by his science first seduced the modern world, the Heavenly Almighty agreed to allow his absolute dominion over all the world in return for his promise never to meddle in matters of heavenly concern; from which it follows that nothing spiritual is to be allowed to thrive on Earth. But an amazing rumor has reached the Almighty that spiritual beings are at large in New Zealand in Mr. Salter's vast mountain forest.

Gabriel, who has long since ceased to be the magnificent young angel of the Annunciation and now appears as a doddering old man in a bedraggled robe, potters about among the trees and soon announces that he can hear the singing of elemental spirits, "births of the random growths and kissing air," near a waterfall. But Lucifer tells him not to worry; he boasts that, thanks to his sciences, no man on earth today has either ears or eyes for such apparitions, and so the treaty will stand. Nevertheless, he considers it expedient that the forest be destroyed, and to accomplish this he transforms himself into Mr. Bishop, the lumber merchant, first to gain Mrs. Salter's support and through her to put pressure on Salter to sell.

Thus we are shown both the origin and the results of that divorce between Heaven and Earth, between the spiritual and the
material, between Man and his true place in Nature. Modern man
faces a dilemma. No matter how earnestly he may incline to
abstract spiritual pursuits or, if his bent is otherwise, to enjoyment
of material possessions, he is doomed to frustration and unhappi-
ness because all those former harmonies have been destroyed.
Gross materialism takes the place of physical Nature, while
"holy anaemia," as the poet in the play puts it, passes for spiritual-
ity. Poor old Gabriel thinks regretfully of a time on this Earth

> in its happy prime
> When men and we, like playful little boys,
> Ran in and out of one another's doors
> And hardly lived at home.

Cresswell writes much of the play's humor into this first act,
into the byplay between anemic old Gabriel (who is almost a
figure of fun as such a being would be to the modern man) and
bold and brassy Lucifer, *reasonable* Lucifer (as the Devil is re-
spected in the modern world by men such as Bishop). There are,
too, many sharp thrusts at today's trends and institutions. On
war, for example:

> *Gabriel* (to Lucifer): We thought in Heaven these wars
>   were your devising.
> *Lucifer*: Men think so too. But I detest these wars.
> Peace, Gabriel, so that wickedness can thrive,
> That's what I want . . .
> *Gabriel*: Whence come these wars then, Lucifer?
> *Lucifer*: I'll tell you.
> My hold is on men's reasons, as I've said.
> 'Tis fastened there by strange contrivances:
> Inventions, engines—no need to tell you what.
> But fast as I corrupt men with these toys,
> Nature, from that wild past within them still,
> So clouds their reasons, mingles with their dreams
> Such dreadful memories of that underworld,
> As makes them turn these toys to monstrous arms
> And fight among themselves. She'll stop at nothing
> To turn me out. And nor will I to stay here.
> *Gabriel* (aside): Alas, poor Devil! He gives men aeroplanes,

And she makes them see flying saucers! What a World!
Lucifer: She wouldn't care if men lost all they have
And were but naked savages again
If she could loose the hold I have on them
And make them honest as their fathers were.
Two wars in quarter of a century,
And worse to come I fear! Another war
Might put our way of seeing out of fashion
And bring in hers again. But I'm not idle.
And lately, Gabriel, as I believe
I've found a way to make men peaceable:
I've split the atom, sir, a thing so frightful
I'm hopeful men may fear to fight with it.
For if they do 'twill be the end of us;
While peaceably employed, in fifty years
'Twould make this woman's World forever mine.

In Act Three there is a conversation between Gabriel and
George who because he is a poet can, of course, talk with angels.
This scene is used by Cresswell to point to things to come. After
some witty exchanges at the expense of fallen angels and modern
men, George, excited by the voices of forest and waterfall, speaks
his thoughts aloud.

> ... the Sun, whose setting leaves these woods
> To a more seeing darkness, even as the pomps
> And shallow prodigies of modern science
> Shall set, and leave to this tired World
> A holier and a better superstition. . . .
>
> Come, Imagination!
> Come, Truth! There is a better ignorance
> Than blasted knowledge. . . .
>
> You stifled forests, open your swelling pores
> And sweat sweet gums! Let your excited tops
> Signal me when they see the pitch black sail
> Of coming Chaos, bring as it must,
> The god-head to these shores.
> *Gabriel* (aside): New gods! Oh well,
> We've had our day. What can we do but die?
> *George*: Then show me where the *infant* wonder lies
> That I may know his looks and learn his name,

And worship, as the Christian shepherds did
Led by the star of poets.

V   *The Gods Return*

Soon, because of this cooperation of the poet with the Archangel,
and because even *one* true poet is enough to send the Devil packing, Lucifer acknowledges defeat, at least in that hemisphere, and
takes flight to the northern world. This defection leaves Bishop
bereft of his demonic impulse, and he falls dead in a forest glade.
Mrs. Salter takes the car and leaves for the city, swearing never to
return.

In the final scene, Gabriel enters, robed as before, but now
upstanding, purposeful, and rejuvenated. In a ringing youthful
voice he delivers this speech.

> Lucifer's gone!
> And Bishop's dead and gone. But I'll not go.
> For since this golden sun began to rise,
> Its thrilling beams that pierce me through and through,
> Groping for what I was three thousand years
> And more ago, have made me young again.
> I'll not go back where I was Gabriel.
>   (He tears the halo from his head)
> I'll stay on Earth, which had I never left
> I never had grown old.
>   (He throws off his robe, revealing
>   figure of a beautiful young man,
>   naked save for a girdle)
>   With Nature's help
> I'll be the leader of these infant spirits
> Whose nursery is this forest. Night and day
> I'll rear them to do battle with the Fiend
> Who has usurped this World. This poet, too,
> I'll help against dislike and poverty
> Lest Lucifer should harm him. All his days
> I'll love this boy, and every friend of his
> I'll love. And while they live, and when they die,
> Together we'll make war on Lucifer!

These quotations are few enough, but they should show something of the scope of the play. A full reading would prove that

Cresswell manages to translate into concrete and poetic terms, combined with wit and satire, most of the reasoned argument of *Eena Deena Dynamo*. But beyond all this there is something even more interesting: Cresswell's dealing with what might be called the ultimate Christian hopes—a new Heaven and a new Earth, and the return of the Deity. *The Forest* is concerned not so much with *Lyttelton Harbour's* theme of the foundering of the now unseaworthy bark of Christendom as with the promised future; not so much with the return of the Greek-named Pagan gods as with the coming of the as yet unnamed One, as when George exclaims: "Signal me when they see the pitch black sail of coming Chaos bring, as it must, the god-head to these shores." Although George, in the next few lines, asks to be shown where "the *infant* wonder lies," we should remember that he is speaking to Gabriel, traditionally the angel of the Annunciation, and is recalling the manner of Christ's birth in that other advent of the god-head.

Later in the play, when the ancient Gabriel is transformed into a young Apollo-like figure radiant with the risen sun, he announces one who will nurture poets and wage final war on Lucifer. This recalls a passage that Cresswell had written earlier in his Thesis to the effect that, in his second coming, Jesus Christ, "the purest Pagan," would be seen more as the Father of Poets than as the Son of God. This new emphasis on Christian eschatology does not represent a change of outlook for Cresswell, as is made clear in letters to friends, but we may see in it influences of his formal instruction in the Christian faith by a priest of the Church of England, culminating in his confirmation in 1942 by the Bishop of London.

Another way of looking at it is that Cresswell, a man who endeavored to harmonize all things, especially all extremes, is at this period of his progress deliberately recreating the harmony between the Classical Pagan and the Christian. He restates his belief that the coming civilization will be a synthesis of the two, with a leaning to the concrete and polytheistic once more, just as pre-Reformation Christendom was at heart such a synthesis, but with a strong leaning to the abstract and monotheistic. Now Man must learn to use his eyes again, to look and see created things, because

> The seeing eyes of men, sir, are put out
> Since [Lucifer] took charge of this successful world. . . .
>
> Nothing's in vogue now that's not reasonable,
> And reason, if a man gets drunk on it,
> Is deadly to the sight. . . .
>
> It's a poison, sir, which strengthens in proportion.
> But taken neat, it blinds him at arm's length
> While flattering him he sees interminably.

It is interesting to compare the passage given above with the words attributed to Jesus Christ by Saint Matthew to explain his speaking to men in parables, that is to say, in poems. He quotes a prophecy of Isaiah:

> You will listen and listen again, but not understand,
> see and see again, but not perceive.
> For the heart of this nation has grown coarse,
> their ears are dull of hearing, and they have shut their eyes,
> for fear they should see with their eyes,
> hear with their ears,
> understand with their heart,
> and be converted [that is, changed]
> and be healed by me.[3]

Nothing there about relying on pure reason. See with the eyes, understand with the *heart;* a perfect prescription to heal the ills of our times.

It was with these high matters thus truly established in fact that Cresswell a little later, in 1948, wrote the memoir *Margaret McMillan,* which we looked at in our Introductory chapter. In that unique biography, he was able vividly to portray a noble character in the modern world, one in whom there was that blend of the perceptive mind and the heart; an ardent spirit, poetic and prophetic, a social idealist, and a tireless and practical worker for man's better material condition, all in one. With that work of lively prose Cresswell rounded off a period in his literary life.

CHAPTER 5

The World Rejected

I Final Farewell

CRESSWELL'S last major poem is *The Voyage of the Hurunui: a Ballad.* Early in 1950 Cresswell set out for New Zealand, his aged and ailing father having expressed a wish to see his youngest son. Without means, he sought aid from the New Zealand State Literary Fund Committee which eventually granted it on condition that he use the time of the journey to work on a poem of some length and substance. He was able to secure a passage on the refrigerated cargo ship *Hurunui*, aboard which he would be the only passenger.

Cresswell also half hoped to find, at last, honor among his fellow countrymen, and the means to live there suitably and continue to write poetry. He was now without employment in England, and the promise of recognition there had faded. Moreover, he was now in his fifties and reluctant to face the grimmer hardships of his younger days. But he was quite unprepared for the coldness of his reception in New Zealand. Only the companionship of a handful of his old friends helped him bear up.

On the ship's arrival at Wellington he went straightaway to Lyttelton Harbour where he found his father living at Governors Bay. It was a short visit, and must have been painful for both; it was the last time he was to see his father alive. He continued aboard the *Hurunui* as far as Auckland where he found a little oasis of friendship, and Lindsay Fraser, the painter, lodged him in his studio. It was at Frank Sargeson's cottage nearby that he read to his friends his as yet unpublished play, *The Forest*. Soon after, Bob Lowry began printing it at his Pelorus Press.

Apart from his friends, he soon found his name and his overseas exploits almost forgotten, even by those who should have had the cause of letters most at heart. Now all chance of suitable employment seemed lost; and he suffered much pinpricking and coldness besides. So he visited all the New Zealand ports that the ship put in to, and returned on her to England and a gloomy future. No wonder he swore never again to set foot on his native land! Never, at least, until he was begged to come; and then only to a suitable station in life.[1]

On the ship he began a poem, as the Literary Fund people had demanded of him: *The Voyage of the Hurunui.* It was not published however, until 1956, in New Zealand, only a few years before his death. In the Foreword, Cresswell attempted to disarm those critics who would rail loudest against his style. He wrote:

As for the style of the poem, the many rhymes and incessant metres, the evident echoes and archaisms, the 'I wis' and 'full sore' and all that, I am heartily glad of them. I hold that a poet may, and will, use just what words and measures he pleases, however far-fetched, from the past. Fashionable verse-making was never my aim. I have never worked for that market, to whose loose, slangy uproar (now a little abated) I am happily stone-deaf, whether by choice or by nature. I never hear it when I sit down to write, but only that other wild, unchanging music, with its unsearchable silences, on which I eavesdrop, which bids me write as I feel and in whatever terms I prefer. It is only thus that poetry takes root in the poet's heart, and strikes upward and demands all his care and attention until its strange conclusion appear, whatever that be. . . .

As for the theme of the poem, the narrator is supposed to be a well-educated able seaman. But he must not be supposed to be addressing his shipmates aloud, except for an occasional verse in italics about doings on deck or below as the ship nears land. The rest, although at times addressed to the captain and men of the crew, is "locked fast inside the cowardly fellow's head, a fanciful going *backwards* which at times gets sadly entangled with all which is actually going *forward*." For the ship, in the intoxicated imagination of the narrator, is fleeing from land while in fact she is nearing land after a six months' voyage.

II   *New World and Old*

Homeward bound and outward bound,
'Twixt the New Isles and the Old,
We've trailed our log through sun and fog
And cared for heat nor cold.

Outward bound and homeward bound
From the Old Isles to the New
And back again to these crowded Isles
Is twenty and four thousand miles
And I've loved each man of you.

But shipmates, if you see landfall
There's nothing I can say.
Unless you see deep down like me
We must part, alas, this day![2]

These stanzas, in some ways at least, reflect Cresswell's own situation on the *Hurunui* as he worked at the poem while returning to England. *His* spirit, too, feared the approaching shore and harked back to the far Southern land to which, nevertheless, he knew he was not now free to return. This was, he realized, the inevitable end of his voyaging to and fro, to the Old World from the New. But he had accomplished much.

I'm not the man I was before
Since a spirit I have seen
On farmer watch, on the for'ard hatch,
A spirit like a lighted match,
And the black sea changed to green!

Now he knows that the Old is doomed, while the New is yet a promised land; still deep in the Hades of the South waiting to be reborn. In that promised land he can live only in spirit.

. . . And I saw great wonders in God's name
Though there wasn't any sun.

I saw this World with its walls and towers,
And the World's foundations split,
And the World fell flat. And after that
The deep flowed over it.

And the World was gone. But the thin sea shone
   As if the sun rose under
On another world which there had birth
Like a new Heaven and a new Earth
   And I saw deep down with wonder!

This sea-cock leaks like it's done for weeks.
   The thread's in bad condition.
We fixed that light in the mess all right
   You can tell the Electrician.

Cresswell's task was a lifelong attempt to harmonize the inherited
culture of the Old World with the fresh vigor of the New World.
Both had to be purified in spirit; for the one was contaminated by
a stale and sickly sophistication, the other by rank materialism.
Now the attempt at harmony, the broad statement, is transferred
to poetic terms. The shining spirit speaks to the sailor:

"For you are he whose soul I be,
   "For each man hath a soul
"Though it dwell more far than the sunk day-star
   "Below the wintry Pole. . . . "

"The World's high towers are no longer ours,
   "We are outlaws in men's sight
"Since they drove us out with lies and doubt
"To the wild sea-waves and the winds without,
   "To the depth and to the height."

"The World's high towers are no longer ours,
   "We are past as a time that's past.
"But time doth bring like an endless ring
   "All first things to be last. . . . "

"Oh, beware landfall where the Fiend rules all
   "And the Devil hath his throne!
"For I'll rise no more if you step on shore
   "Ere your faith to me is shown.
"Till the work is done which makes us one
"If you land you land alone!

"He rules Mankind through the abstract mind,
   "Through a false abstract ideal.
"To a god untrue he maketh you
   "And all Mankind to kneel,

"To an unreal whole which I your soul
      "Nor see nor hear nor feel.
"For the Beautiful made visible
      "Through the sensual parts, Love's citadel,
"Alone is true and real. . . . "

"Then out! Put out! Put the ship about
      "From this wicked World I urge ye!
"When the Fiend the reason doth refine
"The senses to the mire decline
"And the heart in darkness doth repine,
"Though the physicist and the scholar shine
      "For they're the Devil's clergy!"

Not that rope, son, the other one.
      Can you hear me up aloft?
Let her down a bit—that one, that's it.
      Well I'm damned, the fellow's daft!

III *A Spell on Science*

And what of the many repetitions? Cresswell insists that if the
"imaginary" voyage, and the reasons for it, was to be seen in
proper perspective beside the real voyage, and the reasons for
that, then his account of the matter could not be one line less prolonged; and he believed that the many repetitions in the circumstances were vital to the spell-making intention of the poem.
Spell-making intention, mark you; a deliberate intent to use ritual
incantation, as distinct from merely rational argument, as a means
to his end.

Out! out! Put out! Put the ship about!
      Oh, I fear we are too late!
For the Engineer hath a fair young bride,
Though her lips are false and her nails are dyed
Yet he knows no god nor good beside
And he's sworn that he will catch the tide
      And we're nigh at London Gate! . . .

Though a married wife be a joy for life
      There are those whose love is stronger
Than wife's or bride's, whom the winds and tides
And the waves tell of and the deep sea hides,
      And these have waited longer.

> Though a married wife be a joy for life
>   As I have heard men say,
> *Their* love, it said at my bunkhead,
> Outlasts the living and the dead,
> And a man's no man till he be wed
>   Forever and for aye!

Then out! put out! Put the ship about (etc.)

Regarding the "evident echoes" mentioned in the Preface, the most obvious echo, of course, comes straight from *The Rime of the Ancient Mariner*, a fact on which critics have picked only to disparage this poem by comparison with that. But the intentions are different. In *The Ancient Mariner*, the crime of destroying the Albatross, the spirit of Nature, is the crime of a rebellious or ignorant individual who yet involves, partly because of their neglect to chide him, the members of his community. In the end the punished and now penitent individual attempts to warn others of the danger of this rebellion against Nature, but is not heeded. So the crime is multiplied and infects society which itself becomes the murderer. In *The Voyage of the Hurunui* the now guilty society, criminal in the intensity of its rebellion against Nature, involves even every innocent individual, no matter how he may protest. The only remedy now left the innocent is to "flee the shore where the Fiend holds sway"; that is, to prepare to welcome, on "the deep," the deep-sea Pilot.

Cresswell uses all the "echoes" to reinforce *his* meaning. Now the ship, in the fevered imagination of the seaman, is sailing south again, saving him, and almost against their wills, his companions from the condemned World "where the Fiend reigns."

> Each day more high in the blazing sky
>   As southward we shall steer
> We'll watch him [the sun] rise and we'll see him set
> Till the smooth sea shines, as if not wet,
> Like a molten ore, but it won't be yet
>   That Pilot will appear. . . .

> [But] when man or mast no shadow cast,
>   When the huge sky weighs like lead,
> When the sea's shrunk so you could almost row

Right round—that day, it said,
We shall see a sign as we cross the Line
As the sun sinks round and red.

As that sun shall sink in the ocean's brink
On its round red disc we'll see
From the upper deck a small black speck
Like an unknown rock or a lost shipwreck:
Praise God, it will be he! . . .

The deep-sea Pilot, it is he
Who never plies near land,
And that wondrous light 'tis our spirits bright
That close beside him stand.
And his fiery wake more spirits make
Who follow in his band.
But his face is dark as his lampless bark[3]
And awful to command!

Aye, aye, Bosun! I've made her fast.
We'll be in at three? That's swell.
There's not enough paint for the for'ard mast
Tell Lamps—and the winch as well.

The *Voyage of the Hurunui* is a continuation of *The Rime of the Ancient Mariner*. But now all is strangely reversed to be true in this age. The Ancient Mariner beheld the death-ship and saw his companions die in mid-ocean, and only later was he rescued and taken to his native shore by a seeming human pilot. The sailor of the *Hurunui* thinks to flee from the Fiend ashore and encounters the supernatural deep-sea Pilot south of the Line. He and his sailor companions are given new life, but the Captain— commander under the Devil's orders—is struck dead, and the Engineers only win a reprieve after a purgatory and after abandoning their engines.

In both poems there is a Wedding, symbol of union and harmony, of men with Nature, of man with society, and eventually, of man with Spirit. In the first poem, the Wedding-guest, the recipient of the Mariner's confidences, is constantly prevented from joining the Marriage Banquet, and at the end of the narrative, the invited Guest turns away from the Bridal door like a stricken being; a vivid picture of Man in our times, knowing in his heart of hearts that he is the invited guest, but grief-stricken because of his rejection of that invitation and thus an outcast from the joy of the Banquet. "Turn away no more, why wilt thou turn away?" another poet, William Blake, cried to willful man.

In Cresswell's poem, on the other hand, we are given a glimpse of that promised harmony and unity of Man and Spirit under a new Heaven, on a new Earth.

> And the sun will rise in the clear blue skies,
>   And we all on deck will stay,
> And we'll feel no heat on hands or feet
> Nor thirst to drink nor faint to eat
>   Though we stand there all that day.
> And the ship beneath us on that sea
> Will stand as if bewitched, as we.
> Ten days she'll stand like a rooted tree
>   Though her engines pound away.

But there are conditions before Man is free to go and enter the promised land.

> And thus we'll stay. For it [his soul] did say
>   Till our engine-crew below
> Shall hark as well to that Pilot fell
>   And turn their backs on the engine-bell
> That their souls may enter them as well
>   We will no further go.

When our mad engineers and technicians submit to the commands of the Pilot, or are forced to submit by disillusioned men and by dire events, how sweet life will be!

> It's good to lie 'neath the open sky
>   On a day that's warm and fair,
> To leave behind the darkened mind,
>   The cause of all our care,
> With the senses free to hear and see
> What pleasant sights and sounds there be
>   In earth and sea and air.

But they will no longer eat shipboard food; at sunrise and sunset "five spirits fair" will bring them the food man most hungers for. We are given a picture of this new communion:

Five hatches that are low and flat
    We have, and white as snow
Each will be spread with heavenly bread
And fruits whereon are angels fed
    Like none on Earth which grow.
And these we'll eat, and nectar sweet
We'll drink, as bright and cold as sleet
    Which only spirits know.

And when we eat of that spirit meat,
    Unlike the foods that rot,
Our bodies they will be as air
    Though each man knows it not.
And nothing will grieve nor harm us there,
For wives and sweethearts we will not care.
    This World will be forgot . . . .

And we behold with our spirits' eyes
Not the winking sun where he doth rise
But a wondrous god who walks the skies,
And voices we shall hear likewise
From the air and from the sea.

IV *For the Fiend Defeat?*

After this vision there follows a lengthy sequence in which the
spirits discuss with the seaman's soul the traitorous tricks of fallen
reason which the Devil used to establish his reign over mankind
and to strengthen his dominion. Nevertheless, it appears, Man is
given the means to overthrow that tyranny and to become free
again, and at peace with himself and with God. It is really an
incantatory form of that large statement which Cresswell continued to affirm during his lifetime in other forms, in both prose
and poetry.

This sequence reviews the birth of words, engendered by Man's
cry of adoration wrung from him when first he heard the One
Word in the great silence of created things; and of the beginning
of reason therefrom. It also recounts Man's discovery, when his
senses were excited by the visual light of Nature, of the dark
wonder of the Abstract Light. From these marvels, Man learned
to rejoice in the coming of the Splendour—but not in mere parts
such as leaves or flowers or the varied lights of Nature, because

"not direct but as these reflect can Beauty's self be seen," whose other names are Truth and Love.

What was once done in the beginning shall be done anew to free mankind from the Fiend's grip. We see here Cresswell wielding yet another and newly forged weapon, making his final major thrust at the Enemy, his last effort as champion of mankind.

> The food we eat will be rare and sweet
>   That each man liketh best
> As on we glide without wind or tide
>   And neither east or west.
>
> The food we eat will be rare and sweet
>   That melts in each man's mouth
> As on we glide with our souls inside
>   And neither north nor south. . . .
>
> The ship will be invisible
>   As she floats on a still, clear sea.
> The ship will be invisible
> From her poop to her forepeak's hanging bell
> From her samson posts to her long, low hull,
>   Invisible as we. . . .

Next his spirit speaks to him of how he shall cherish his five senses; they shall be her instruments to defeat the Fiend:

> 'For by these alone may the gulf be flown
> 'That fatal is to flesh and bone
> 'If beauty they have seen and known
> 'Though the erring mind should perish.'
>
> ' And with these five the mind doth thrive,
>   'With these, and these alone.
> 'In the Beautiful made visible
> 'Doth the Word take flesh on Earth to dwell,
> 'And the senses five are Her citadel
>   'Which the Fiend hath overthrown. . . . '

Then the seaman meditates on all he has been told.

> Oh, strange! oh, deep as death or sleep!
>   Too deep, too strange to tell. . . .

[Then] the concrete parts their dark disguise
Will shed, and the abstract Sun will rise,
One splendour of earth, seas and skies,
        As all the parts unite,

As the spirit peers through the eyes and ears
And the joyful heart now sees and hears
        All things as beauty bright!

Christ on Earth was "the Word taken flesh"; Christ risen, but invisible, is "the abstract Sun" of Christendom. On his coming again "the abstract Sun will rise," and then "the concrete parts their dark disguise will shed," and will manifest Divinity. Man will no longer grub vainly for the secret of matter but will rejoice in the newly revealed secret of life.

You'll see it clear as you see me here,
        As if the sun rose under
On another World which there had birth
Like a new Heaven and a new Earth
You'll see deep down with wonder!

But the poor fellow keeps remembering that the ship *hasn't* put about; that it is all the time nearing land.

But away! away! What do I say!
        Oh, we are too late! too late!
We are round the Nore where either shore
Leads in to London Gate!

Oh, I'll never land though it be at hand.
        If you won't turn round I say
On a dolphin's back along our track
        I'll be gone ere break of day,
For I hear the band on Margate sand
        And the Devil's tune they play!

There are but two (great) works can do
        And the Devil he is one,
And the other's God and His Holy Ghost
        And we know how *their* works were done.
And they are not seen in *this* World I ween
        Nor yet His blessed Son.

> We're off Gravesend, Jock, did you say?
> Mud-pilot's come aboard?
> No thanks, old chap, I won't need a strap,
> I'll carry it by the cord.

Even now the seaman knows that escape is possible if only the Captain and the crew listen to his warning. And with his mind's eye he sees the delights that await those bold enough to put about and shame the World; to submit to the deep sea Pilot and defeat the Fiend.

> Off Plymouth Bay we can be ere day
>   And I know what will befall
> When we all shall rise as drowned men rise
> To the ship that far above us lies
> To the weed that swims and the fish that flies,
> When we've seen deep down with these two eyes,
>   For last night it told me all. . . .
>
> By day and night in the sun so bright
> And the large round moon with a new delight
> We'll frisk and play, for we've put to flight
>   The Fiend who plagues us sore. . . .
>
> Transparent whales with threshing tails
>   Will come if we do call,
> And we shall ride their backs astride
>   And never fear to fall,
> For the saltless "brine" will taste like wine
>   And we can swim withal!
>
> But ask me not why in sea and sky
>   With fishes large and small
> And the moon so bright, like a sun at night,
>   These marvels will befall. . . .
>
> But we'll see deep down and we will not drown
>   When the World's foundations split
> And the World falls flat and after that
>   The deep flows over it.
>
> We'll see deep down and we will not drown
>   When the World's high towers shall fall,
> When the strange green flash, like a lightning flash
> Leaps upward from its last red ash

> As the World goes down without a splash,
>   For we can swim withal.
>
> Then out! put out! Turn right about!
>   Oh, now we are too late. . . !
>
> *What, Albert Docks? Hell, where's my socks!*
>   *So long, Butch, don't get tight!*
> *Give my regards to your mum and dad.*
> *Yes, I'll bring Doris if you'll bring Glad.*
>   *We'll be round on Saturday night.*

Even on the very eve of the ship's landfall, however, his spirit's words and warnings continue to haunt him, with only the spirit's strange promise to give him hope:

> "And when you and we, as we'll surely be,
>   "Are soul and sense again,
> "In time forlorn, in a World outworn
>   "By man's overweening brain,
> "In that hour of dearth of our sensual mirth
> "The fallen World shall have rebirth
> "Though the snow lie deep on the darkened earth
>   "And the ice its streams enchain."

Thus, the poem ends in a way as somber and almost as fearful as *The Rime of the Ancient Mariner,* but now the Guest knows that eventually he will enter and partake of the Banquet.

At the time of the poem's appearance in New Zealand in 1956, it received scant notice and little commendation; perhaps less than any other of Cresswell's works. Critics and reviewers either ignored it or paraded a host of faults and objections. In spite of some groups of fine lines, one wrote, it was a dull and depressing performance.[4] Cresswell was accused of sermonizing, but one could not understand his preaching or find any meaning in whole stanzas, the critics claimed. And anyway, the whole thing could be written off as poetry since it was composed almost entirely in clichés. To which last criticism we may reply that Cresswell tells us that the narrator "must be supposed a well-educated able-seaman." And is it not a commonplace that today's "well-edu-cated" think almost entirely in clichés?

No one followed the clue of the "many echoes," or considered in what particular way *The Hurunui* followed or continued *The Ancient Mariner,* or in what ways it is related to Cresswell's other works. Perhaps we should make some allowances for the critics. For the mind which has been molded (brainwashed, I believe is the modern term) by the modern world and *its poets,* there is difficulty in understanding Cresswell's poetic attitudes and intentions, and in appreciating his truth to "one course" from the sonnets of *Lyttelton Harbour,* through the blank verse of *The Forest,* to the ballad style of *The Hurunui.* To one not familiar with, or antipathetic to Cresswell's prose philosophy the long conversation in the middle of the poem between the souls of the seamen and the spirits of sea and air, is likely to be a source of bafflement or of irritation.

In answer to the charge that the whole thing shows only Cresswell's failing poetic powers and dullness of ear, allied to carelessness and unintelligibility verging on nonsense, we should recall that the poem was written by a man who had only recently completed *The Forest.* The dates of publication of the two works are no guide in this matter. Cresswell put the final touches to *The Forest* after he made his last voyage to New Zealand on board the *Hurunui,* and it was on the return voyage to England later the same year that he wrote most of the ballad which bears the name of the ship.

It is now admitted by the critics that *The Forest* is a major poetical achievement. As one critic wrote: "The verse is fully developed, sustained throughout and finished with a technical precision achieved only by our best short story writers but by no poet in a work of any length. . . . In Cresswell's blank verse we hear the authentic accents of an original poet."[5] Then is it believable that, in a matter of months, the same poet, during the same voyage, would be bereft of his powers, his precision, and the sharpness of all his senses? No, we can only conclude that Cresswell meant precisely what he wrote, in the way that he wrote it. Sonnets and verse of a much later date show no failing of the poet's power, as we shall see.

It is hoped that the passages from *The Hurunui* selected for this study, together with the suggested interpretation, may help the reader understand something of Cresswell's versatility, of his swift changes of mood and armament, Proteus-like, against the single Enemy. That One it is meant to baffle. If, at the moment, we find the work somewhat baffling to modern ears, let us think of it as Cresswell's secret weapon!

CHAPTER 6

And by the World Reviled

I The Last Decade

L ET us now consider the significance of the last ten years of
the poet's life. Cresswell returned from New Zealand to London a disappointed man, no longer young, with no means and no
prospects. His influential friends in England were dead or had
now forgotten him. His uncompromising view of poetry became
increasingly more unpopular; it was frankly distasteful to a world
turning more and more to its material preoccupations, in which
scientific thought became ever more abstract, as also did the very
forms of living. The manner in which this influenced the arts was
readily accepted by most of Cresswell's contemporaries, but to
these he would not allow the title of poet. They, however, had
access to the paying markets of what is now called "mass media";
Cresswell's work remained unpublished.

About this time he wrote in a letter to two friends[1] that, after
a night of prayer to his Providence, it had been shown him what
he must do. That was to attack in satires all those he named false
poets, have these verses printed, and tramp the roads selling them
as once before, in his youth, he had done, although now he was
aging and weary. He proceeded with this plan, writing satires
whenever a good idea occurred to him. Not long after, he was
offered work as night-watchman in a government office building,
Somerset House, in London—work which would enable him to
keep his cottage in St. John's Wood and have means to live fru-
gally and even to pay for the printing of some of his poems. Also
it would leave enough time to continue writing. He looked on this
humble job as literally a godsend. But, pacing the dark and lonely

building by night and attending to household chores in his secluded cottage by day, seldom going abroad except to work or to buy food, he became lonelier and felt ever more rejected. It was indeed in many ways a monastic life—monastic in its poverty, in its silent aloneness, in its absolute dedication to the task his conscience imposed.

It is from these years of aloneness when, at times, he almost despaired of his task, that come such verses as:

> The moon is up, the lamp is low
> O suffering Christ where shall I go!
>
> I cannot in this cottage stay
> Either by night now, or by day.
>
> Is there no rock nor cave nor tree
> In all this World will shelter me?
>
> *There is no rock nor cave nor tree*
> *In all this World will shelter thee.*
>
> *There is no rock nor tree nor cave*
> *Will thee from thy great glory save:*
> *A lonely life, a poet's grave!*[2]

And this Epitaph, titled R.I.P.:

> D'Arcy Cresswell was my name,
>   New Zealand was my nation,
> London was my dwelling place
>   And *drink* was my probation.
>
> Love was my guide. 'Twas he who cried
>   At every door "Take me inside!"
> I did, and we were *crucified,*
>   And this was my salvation.[3]

Now that he had a frugal living assured, at least for the immediate future, he used some of his wages to pay a printer to print a selection of his satirical verses under the title of *Poems for Poppycock*. This was issued by The Trireme Press, as he named his little publishing venture. Not that he sold many copies; they mostly went to his friends and to various literary celebrities and editors in England and overseas. From some of those people he received notes expressing polite interest, disapproval, or faint amusement. From most there was no reply—or else curt displeasure. No wonder, when we consider the name and fame of many of those he parodied. The great modern "cultured public" does not like to be told that those it has elected to the role of gods—even merely literary gods—are not even wholly intelligent mortals. And, anyway, "literature," having become deadly serious nowadays, may not be laughed at! Things like this were not appreciated:

> If Mr. Eliot and I
> Were looking at the sea
> His clever mind would reasons find
> For calling it a tree.
> And every critic in his train
> Would eagerly agree.

Or this, "Overheard at Delphi":

> Say, Goddess, what's the most profound
> Dark riddle of the Age, I crave 'e?
> "A poem by Mr Ezra Pound
> "Reviewed by Mr Donald Davie!"

There are poems of this period, though, in which a brave poetic spirit speaks to men of spirit in other lands, rebuking those who remain silent regarding injustice. When powerful England began to suppress by force of arms the Greek Cypriot movement towards unity with Greece, Cresswell alone among English poets made his voice heard. Cresswell braved the anger and contempt of influential sections of the British public and the very real risk of imprisonment for sedition. Not one of his contemporaries appeared aware of England's public shame, her betrayal of championship of freedom. It was very unlike the dutiful chorus aroused by the nightmare of Spain. Altogether he published some dozen sonnets under the general title of *Poetry in Cyprus: A Manifesto for Moderns. Eoka* is a typical example.

> Are they not Greeks? Does not their courage show
> These Cypriots are the old heroic breed

That dared defy the myriads of the Mede
And saved the world for Freedom? Even so.
Stir that dead fire and still its ashes glow!
Murderers you call them, terrorists indeed!
Bare-fisted patriots rather, who but need
Arms in their hands to bring you English low
And hurl you from the island! Wanting these,
Stealth is their only weapon and surprise,
The bullet in the back! If terror lurk
On every crag in Cyprus, till there lies
For traitors no safe road but overseas,
That's England's and her minion Harding's work.

And this: *They When in Irons.*

'Two British women shot in Cyprus!' Stay!
How many German women did you kill
On joyous midnights when the moon was full?
What scruples had you when you stood at bay,
Your liberties inviolate as today,
The invader distant and invisible?
No German sergeants' wives in Notting Hill!
You found them even so. And so did they
Whose isle you cram with troops, annul its laws,
Arrest, gaol, hang and govern by decree.
'Two British women shot, and without cause'.
Worse cause, and readier pardon than for ye!
You did the same while England was yet free,
They when in irons, and those irons yours!

To this brave advocacy of freedom, this cry in defense of heroic
people, the only official reaction was the threat of imprisonment;
a threat only stayed, perhaps, because Cresswell was a New
Zealander. And from the general public, apathy.

. . . oh, what a name you English throw away,
Whom Fame for her most cherished garland chose—
To rescue Hellas in her darkest day,
When Greece to Shelley's thrilling music rose
And Byron's rousing and impassioned lay.
Would the World now had voices such as those!

But he did receive honor from Archbishop Makarios, and from a few others who mattered.

It was in those years too that Cresswell's sorrow, if not anger, was aroused by the sight of Christopher Marlowe's neglected grave in Deptford churchyard. Marlowe's poetry had made a deep impression on him, especially that poem so prophetic of the tragedy of the modern world, *Doctor Faustus*. Before Marlowe's time, English poets had piped their delightful pastorals; but dark and brooding Marlowe looked beyond all that, and a new poesy was born. Kit Marlowe was the dawn, Cresswell tells us, before Shakespeare's rising sun. Cresswell's long poem *Leander* is his tribute to that dawn. Here are some of the opening verses:

> The morning's songsters are the soonest mum,
> Noisy at dawn, by sunrise they are dumb.
> So with Leander, he was one of those
> Who open early and as early close.
>
> Ere Shakespeare spoke this boy was out of bed
> Whistling to bright Orion overhead.
> He needs no other fact his fame to shout
> Who dared be up before the sun was out!
>
> So bold a thing has never since been known
> As to be up so early and alone
> (Unless it be to venture out of door
> After that sun, as Marlowe did before?).
>
> Like April's before June's his music was,
> Noisy with prophecies which came to pass.
> He saw the way, he sighted the new sea,
> Then left to Shakespeare the discovery.
>
> On shepherd pipes till then our poets played,
> In wistful fairylands their wars were laid.
> Leander scorns to babble on a reed
> While Asia is in flames and towns like rivers bleed.

II   *The Mechanism of Spirit*

It may be said that all Cresswell's work from the sonnets of *Lyttelton Harbour* to *The Forest* and on to *The Voyage of the Hurunui* and these later poems was the fruit of his labor on his *Thesis*, thirty years before in New Zealand. In the Introduction we promised ourselves that in the Conclusion we would spend some little time studying that *Thesis*; but now that we have arrived, having on the way sampled that fruit, all of which is the essence and lively spirits drawn from Nature's soil by the hidden roots of the *Thesis*, does there remain a great need to discover how the seed was winnowed, how the soil tilled and the planting done?

Yet, as it stands, the *Thesis* is such an intriguing piece of prose, with such skillful condensation or distillation of its subject matter, and such compelling logic to lead one purposefully to the conclusion, that we should look into it a little; for all that followed its writing is of another world from that which went before. Listen how majestically its argument begins, like some everlasting gospel, or "good news," as indeed it is. Part One is called Induction; it begins with Man's Creation and Providence.

Formerly all things were of one divine ancestry and marriage of matter and Spirit, whereon the eyes of Mankind were only opened since birth to know Nature its mother (which is wherein matter and Spirit are one) but ever shut on that fearful mystery whereby Spirit created matter before. Thus by instruction of Nature we know what we are and whence descended, but may not lawfully consider how nor deny whence we come. Which were the mutiny of our concrete and abstract faculties and doubt of that supernatural issue and near relation in Nature whereby they arose.

2. Nature's care of Man's Wholeness and Safety. Nature is only Man's nurse and governess, or that mortal condition whereto he is born, whereby Man is reared in the knowledge and love of Spirit his heavenly parent. For as Man honours Nature his earthly parent, so Nature provides him with certain means whereby to know Spirit his heavenly parent. Not to know Spirit itself, which we cannot know; but to know wherein Spirit appears and is present in her. Which is not knowing Spirit, but knowing Spirit to be. And the means wherewith Nature provides us to this end are parts, that provide us wherewith to know Spirit and whole, which we cannot know for ourselves. Which parts of Nature, unless they be shown what they are, or their proof and speaking of Spirit, would hide Man forever from Spirit, and all would be lost. But there is implanted in Man, besides his senses wherewith he knows parts, a certain knowledge of wherein all parts speak of Spirit and whole. Which is spirit in Man. Which highest of our faculties and oneness with Spirit our Maker is whereby this danger of our senses and downfall from Spirit in parts is overcome.

3. Sets out to tell how poets and artists provide us with symbols and words.

And all under artists and poets, who by the affinity of their spirits with all sensible parts see in each part some strangeness of being more than our normal senses can see, which is its import or meaning to be Spirit and whole, or looking towards us of Spirit through sensible parts. Which is only how we get words and come to reason therewith, whereby this care of our spirits and wakefulness of our senses have a voice and remembrance in all affairs of our lives. For poets and artists are beings to whom a mountain is more mountainous, a flower more flower-like, a man more manlike, a god more godlike than to other men, and in all things more sensible, that by their fine faculties they alone give their burden of meaning to all things in Nature that deliver us symbols and words. Which meaning is the wholeness of each thing in itself, which is form, and the total wholeness or harmony of all things together, which is Nature, or matter and Spirit as one. Whereby each thing is pregnant with the import to be Spirit and whole, whether Spirit as mountain, or Spirit as flower, or Spirit as man. And this way all things become words; first that one word which is Spirit ('In the beginning was the Word') and thereafter each sensible thing having import of Spirit as poets perceive. And next by their management of words, poets bring words to that mutual affection and increase of their meaning, or harmony, which is the lawful abstract or wealth thereof, that shows Man to reason or deal in abstract idea; but always in bounds, or having foundation in concrete and sensible fact (which is Nature that keeps us) and in feeling, which is but our affection with sensible fact. . . . And thus symbols and words are Man's whole means of wealth and riches received from Nature his mother, and whereby all greatness and safety of any peoples arise. But only if symbols and words bring us that news and keep that likeness of whence they come. . . .

Having thus shown how true reason arose, Cresswell then set about to show that, because Man is unstable and falls into error, reason comes to reject the restraint of the senses. Finding itself thus without supervision it is soon brought to serve Man's lowest desires in looking away from Spirit to seek some other and op-posite wholeness, which is matter. But matter can never be found by the senses which can only know parts of Nature. Thus, no matter how greatly means are multiplied in the course of these errors, Mankind finds itself in a desert of frustration and impotence where truly men seek bread and find only stones.

There is in *Present Without Leave* a passage where Cresswell describes the problem posed by his view of Mankind's predicament, and how he tackled it.

I had next to show, as my main purpose was, in what manner and by what vain enticement of certainty reason departed from its proper relation with the poetic concrete, in men like Kepler, Galileo and Newton, to encompass a lasting relation with profane and physical matter. . . . But how to show that reason could never, by its nature, encompass the knowledge of matter was a great difficulty, and one that cost me much anguish, as I saw that this must be shown, without which my objections to modern science and doubt of the reality of its Universe was without any foundation. But at last I was able to show the gist of this matter in a few words, how that reason, being only one of our faculties, could of itself know only itself; whereby it left our other faculties and its correspondence therewith in a fallen and derelict state, like its own. (6. How his Reason leads Man Astray.) And next, having shown that reason, ruminating on matter, can discover nothing but itself and get nowhere but where it began, I was able to show that the rational or Copernican Universe was of no more validity than any other view of Nature depending on aberrant and disharmonized faculties; but by stealing words from the true or poetic Universe (whence they came) and perverting symbols and words to its use, it was able to give itself a resemblance to truth. (8. The Perversion of Words to these Errors.) Next I showed how, in a rational Universe wherein our senses take only a subordinate and degraded part, these once equal faculties sink to be only sensation; whereby the division between reason and sense, or abstract and concrete, must perforce become deeper and more fatal still; so that when these faculties meet (as they still meet nevertheless) they meet only unconsciously, propagating together only in darkness, as it were, in an unclean and monstrous connection from which spirit or harmony, that must be looked to in all our affairs, is excluded. (13. How Machines are Begotten, and how they Further Divide our Faculties.) After which I considered by what course of history these things came to be, and to what further course of downfall and penitence they must give rise; and in what manner the harmonized or poetic Universe must be established again.

Having done this, Cresswell thought he should prove the terms he used, so that nothing should be doubted. This he did in the *Synopsis* in a series of axioms each followed by a short passage of proof. He began with the general axiom of all rational inquiry: That which has neither limit nor parts includes that which has limit and parts, as the greater the less. This he followed with that sobering axiom: Spirit is that which has neither limit nor parts. Matter is that which has limits and parts. The apparent contradiction, in reason (that Spirit having neither limit nor parts includes matter which has limit and parts, then Spirit has limit and parts, having matter; which is absurd), he used to demonstrate in a series of further axioms that this which is demonstrably untrue in reason is reversed to be true.

How far he was led, and to what deep matters, is plain from those other axioms, each with its passage of proof. 3. Sense is the action of parts with our senses, and is knowledge of parts. 4. Sensation is sense without mind. 5. Memory or mind is the reaction of sense on parts. (In which he demolished that modern nonsense of "mind over matter" and other like sayings, and insisted that "mind is only memory and the hinge whereon our faculties turn to discover each other.") 6. Abstract or understanding is the relation of parts in mind. 7. Concrete is the relation of parts in sense. 8. Spirit in Man, or identity. In this he showed that there is implanted in Man the faculty of knowing Spirit to be, through the tidings sung by his senses which when in harmony with his reason deliver the true and full import of the multitudinous parts of Nature to speak of Spirit and whole. "And this reversal of concrete and parts to be Spirit and whole is intrinsic Identity, and is whereby this that is demonstrably untrue in reason is reversed to be true." And then, 9. Being public or private (wherein Cresswell informs us that the only right use of symbols and words is to speak of Spirit, which kinds of speech are the only truly public kinds, sharing what all men have in common. But speculation and all else must always remain less than public and mostly private only). 10. Symbols and words are parts as public. 11. Reason is relation of words. 12. Poetry and art are concrete hypothesis. 13 and the next several axioms elaborate on the nature of the arts. Then, 17. Mathematics and number are abstract hypothesis. 18. Science is intrinsic and extrinsic reason in harmony. 19. Religion is the worship of spirit. And, greatly confused today, 20. Private morals are no proper concern of true law.

And all this he did, in his Induction and Synopsis, in fewer than fifty pages. Then, in the Conclusion, he allowed some room to our faculties, "where we can fly about, and come home refreshed." And

if none of the matters viewed in the Conclusion is necessary to the
reasoned argument and proofs of the other two, and even though
some may be thought mere speculation, they are still of moment
and indeed derive their strength from all that goes before—as the
opening sentence shows: "The spirit of Man, where it crouched un-
aware, arose from the feeling and frenzy of poets before visible
things, as Christendom arose from Greece."

III *The Second Coming*

Antiquity and Christendom—those have been the two great civilised and harmonious systems that have gone before. Founded by
artists and poets, as Cresswell points out, or built on their labors,
those systems alone have shown steadfastly the public harmony of
all extremes to be one. Nor will Cresswell allow our present prej-
udices to go unchallenged, but insists that those civilised systems
arose, among the Greeks, by that higher use of their passions
"whereby this love between men was the chief mainstay of those
marvellous times . . ." But, he emphasizes, its present fame with
the lowest shows where *we* are.

This, however, is only one measure of our degradation. Let harmony be lost, in any view of extremes, then the discord spreads to
all, and the downfall of any people begins:

As we see in ancient Greece, how their downfall began between
freedom and slavery, wherein, while a true proportion was kept, they
flourished happily. . . . But pursuing freedom to fantastic extremes,
so as not to trust one another but to waste themselves fighting and
not to combine when they need, they were subdued and made subjects
of the Romans and Barbarians. The Romans fell mainly between
strictness and licence, for while they were temperate and resolute in
themselves they prevailed over all others. But having means to prevail
everywhere, they suppressed all other states and allowed them no
remedy but in revolt, which they welcomed that the enemy might be
severely crushed; as if such extremes should be just. By which lawless
and great aggrandisement the Romans were ruined in their turn. So
with the Christians who next made order out of those vast ruins of
Rome. They were wonderfully stayed a long while between God and
the Devil, and did many excellent things in their lives and works,
as in any happiest nations before; but fell into extremes, and by
abusing that foremost authority they held from God (what none ever

denied them) raised so great objection and bitter rebellion and curiosity as now gives the whole Earth to the Devil. Thus this same harmony that brought that great strength of Antiquity and Barbarianism to be Christendom, now falls to be discord, and must rise from the ground after poets, like the Greeks before. Which is what Christ means by this World passing away and His coming again. In which second coming He shall be found less the Son of God than the father of poets, in the light of this new season and system to come. For Christ was even a poet who mended extremes. Think in what midst of barrenness and stubborn hardness of men He stood, singing parables and feeling poems! His greatest parable was Himself, that He was the Son of God; which the World heard and thirsted after healing in Him. For in a desert men see shining before them what they most need and desire, whether sweet water or shady trees or the Son of God; and this desert stretched over all Asia and fallen Greece and Rome. It is no wonder He rose from the dead and was found divine. Christ harmonises all things, even those things men only saw in their want, which they saw in the fullness of Nature and the wonder of poets before. So that what before was natural now was miraculous. He joins all greatest extremes, the bareness of this World with the mercy of God. He bends and brings all things together and blesses the fulness thereof. He rejoices most over the one that was lost. For the prodigal is the feast. He brings the outcast to the doors of the great. 'Feed my flock.' And 'that is Caesar's but this is God's.' And when no man believed He said 'God is love.' Which is only that oneness which all things desire. And 'consider the lilies.' And 'not a little bird falls.' Which is only mending extremes, where all was torn and at fault. The Jews turned from the living drink of Christ and lost all. But the weary Greeks and Romans received Him, and the hungry Barbarians rushed into his arms. To these Christ was the heart and well-spring of living Nature, the same only law of men's health as poets before, giving life to those strong active limbs. Yet he told them nothing but poems and taught them nothing but harmony, even of life with death. 'Love your enemy.' Which means, love *even* your enemy. This is the sweetest music of extremes among men and perfect embodiment of their health.

We see now that the Christian imagery and viewpoint which, to the surprise of some readers, appeared in Cresswell's later work, such as *The Voyage of the Hurunui*, sprang naturally from the theme that had *always* been Cresswell's preoccupation, the synthesis of Antiquity, polytheistic and concrete, and Christendom, monotheistic and abstract.[4] For it is now obvious that he had always seen the coming order and civilization (announced by poet-prophets and initiated on Earth by a poet-saviour coming again) as a synthesis of those two great former systems, but with a stress now on the concrete and polytheistic rather than on the monotheistic and abstract.

In this respect it is interesting to observe a letter written by Cresswell as early as 1943 to the New Zealand poet Ursula Bethell who had taken him to task for his apparently wishing to reestablish in the world today the ancient Greek paganism with the sacrifice of all that Christianity had since wrought. Cresswell replied:

How quaint that you should think I would substitute Greek and Roman polytheism for Christianity! It will be *our* polytheism, not any antique Greek and Roman. But Christianity keeps the antique beside us, and while that is so I distinguish between these two antiquities, seeing which is the more in keeping with what is to come. . . . In the privacy of our souls there is, and can be, but one god, one source of all. For in the privacy of our souls we depart from matter. But in public life we can nohow depart from matter and nature; as the association of even *two* human beings is bodily, and much more that of millions; and to the fellowship of two beings, nature is at once admitted as a third. This in itself is polytheism . . . just as pure contemplation is monotheism. . . . Public Christianity *was* polytheistic, but of an introvert cast. . . . The whole drift of Christianity is from public to private, extrovert to introvert, polytheism to monotheism; and this is the *Salvation* promised to all who will follow Christ. They are promised to gain private faith notwithstanding that public faith shall *wholly* be lost. Most shall not renounce public sacrilege to this end; but those who do shall be saved. And this introvert mysticism cannot save public life in turn, no matter how many *individuals* are won to Christian introversion; because science, an utterly secular insensitive extroversion, has seized control of public life. But a crude and cruel extrovert worship will begin, and this will be guided by noble minds (the only public path) until on the coming downfall of science mankind will again come into extrovert communion with Divinity.

And he wrote too:

None feel the presence of Christ so nearly as those who feel also his absence from the world; none value his arrival to man like those who mourn his departure, leaving a memory and light in the private heart . . .[5]

But even earlier, in 1933, he had written to a friend:

The Thesis [is] an attempted synthesis of Paganism and Christianity, as the two great stabilised or poetic systems. Christ as the purest pagan and father of poets. . . . This synthesis is a thing I have long dreamed of and wanted through all my being.[6]

It should now be clear how extensive a scope Cresswell's verse attempted to encompass. If, during his lifetime, it failed to convert many to his view of salvation, we need only reflect how few prophets have even been honored in their day, least of all in their own countries. But since his death, events are already pointing to the coming of much that he predicted: youth is everywhere in ferment and united in a kind of supra-lingual mystic internationalism, often practicing a "crude *extrovert* public worship" while rejecting the rational; their conservative elders are driven to irrational hates, or fail with fear, amid the paralysis of their boasted institutions; "repentant" scientists warn mankind of its imminent annihilation through and because of the very technology they once gloried in and cannot stop proliferating; we also witness the increasing irrelevance of political remedies and an instinctive turning toward the anarchic. On the occasion of the ceremonial opening of New Zealand's Parliament in 1968, the official party was swept from the entrance steps by a hostile crowd while a youth unfurled the black banner of Anarchy; a formal intimation, surely, of Cresswell's "approaching dark, devouring Chaos."

It is interesting to observe that now, when a worldwide movement can no longer be ignored, there is building up quite a body of writing examining from within or documenting from without what is becoming known variously as the great freak-out, the underground international, the counter culture, the militant poor, and so on. This body of writing often does little more than catalog and describe; a few writers notice something like a saving vision; others look for ways to give direction to a "movement" whose impetus is always more than a little ahead of these attempts to harness it. Yet fifty years ago, when no one believed him, Cresswell not only foresaw and often discussed the coming of these events, but understood from what deep sources they would spring and recognized what their import would be. Filled with hope he began to place signposts along the way ahead of the present

turmoil and to give us some knowledge of the nature and manner
of the strange new lands to which these events might lead, so
that we be neither lost nor alarmed.

Cresswell must now be seen as the most recent of a long line
of poet-prophets or painter-prophets who have appeared at in-
tervals to warn mankind ever since the world, after the full ripeness of the Renaissance, began ever so gradually at first to fall
into the winter of decay. Such artists are the poet Marlowe in
England and the painter Botticelli in Italy. Such too are the
poets Blake and Coleridge. We have already mentioned Cresswell's admiration for Marlowe, particularly his prophetic *Doctor
Faustus,* and have considered Cresswell's likeness to Blake in
many of his early lyric poems. In his later works we see him
sharing Blake's prophetic note of warning. Blake's warnings were
called madness; yet is there a poem more valid for our times than
The Tiger? All these poetic echoes are found in Cresswell, the
echoes of which he wrote in the *Hurunui* foreword, and which
are never more cogent than his echoes of Coleridge's *Ancient
Mariner.*

IV   *The Vision of Spring*

Perhaps the most notable and interesting parallel is that of
Cresswell with the Italian Renaissance painter Botticelli. Let us
look at three paintings which represent three key periods in Botticelli's life. They are *The Birth of Venus, Primavera* or *Spring,*
and that strange last Nativity so unlike all the many others that
the artist painted, the one now usually known as *The Mystic
Nativity.* Alongside these let us consider Cresswell's *Lyttelton
Harbour, The Forest,* and *The Voyage of the Hurunui.*

When Botticelli painted the *Venus* it was commonly regarded
as an exercise in classicism, much as some regard Cresswell's
invoking of gods and goddesses in *Lyttelton Harbour*—his Phoebus
and horrid satyrs, Hyacinthus and merry Pan. But no great artist,
certainly not Botticelli, harks *back* to the past, although he might
use familiar imagery of a former paradisal age to point his vision
of the *future.* What was Botticelli portraying in that now distant
year of the Renaissance when men were dazzled by a great pour-
ing forth of material wealth and a more scientific learning, when
trade and exploration were thrusting outward the borders of

nations and at the same time creating a new concept of national-
ism, when the cynicism of corruption was already in the air? What
Botticelli painted was the coming on Earth again of the Mother
of Love in a future more joyous Spring. For, at that time, after
a renewal of mankind's spiritual health in a fruitful era of Christendom, an abstract God was receding further and further from
this Earth into an abstract Heaven and becoming ever distant
from men's daily lives which now inclined to paths of commerce,
conquest, discovery, and science.

Pierced by poetic insight into the coming Winter following
the lush Summer of the Renaissance, Botticelli made his vision
clearer and more explicit in his painting of *Spring*. Here Love is
eternally young in possession of a more fruitful Earth. The in-
constant Intellect is now pierced and conquered by the shafts of
Love, and takes a lesser place than the three Graces or Charities,
the perfect embodiment of beauty of body and mind, or the
sensual joys of Flora and the sweet fruits of Spring. Adored by
all is the Mother of Love, now become indistinguishable from
the young and beautiful Christian Mother of God. It is a noble
vision of the reign of Love over a new Earth in a new and lasting
golden age.

In much the same way some of Cresswell's sonnets in his
Lyttelton Harbour were looked on as merely classical conceits
when in fact, having shown the present wreck of the once noble
bark of Christendom, he now really announces (under the Greek
patronymic Phoebus) the coming of a living Sun to burn with
love for Man on a refurbished Earth; a day when the music of
even the cricket or cicada will sound "like morning singing in
the heart of Man." In *The Forest* he has the Satanic Angel, Lucifer, exclaim, "We shall never hear of Heaven again [the *abstract*
Heaven, that is]. Not Heaven, but Nature is my adversary now!"
And when Lucifer takes the guise of the timber merchant Bishop
(that name a symbol of a decadent worldly Church now in un-
holy alliance with worldly commerce) he does so to destroy Nature if he can. In many other passages, as we saw when studying
that poem, Cresswell emphasizes the redeeming role of Nature
and shows us the true relation between love and reason much as
Botticelli does in painting. Cresswell next makes the poet George
cry to the spirit of the forest,

> Signal me when [you] see the pitch black sail
> Of coming Chaos, bring as it must
> The god-head to these shores.

Then, after what must be a time of woes and turmoil,

> Show me where the infant wonder lies
> That I may know his looks and learn his name . . .

In his last years Botticelli became a disciple of Savonarola who
was preaching a change in men's hearts and was setting about
reforming both the Church and the World. From then until his
death he led an austere existence and painted little; but there
is that one great work of this period that has puzzled many: *The
Mystic Nativity* with its cryptic inscription in Greek referring
not to the nominal subject of the painting, the birth at Bethlehem,
but to the woes and the victories prophesied in the Apocalypse.

There is certainly in the central group a portrayal of the Holy
Family, but unlike Botticelli's other sad and pensive Mothers and
solemn Infants, here the Mother's face is radiant with joy and the
Child laughs as he almost leaps from where he lies. Truly this
is "the infant wonder" of Cresswell's poem, a symbol of a new-
born era rather than a mere depiction of a past advent. Look at
the scene above. Three archangels sing *glorias* while in the blue
sky twelve seraphs dance hand in hand swinging olive branches
to and fro and dangling their golden crowns in a wild ecstasy of
joy. What new Heaven is this if not Cresswell's on his mysterious
Voyage?—

> As the Splendour rises from below
> Like the risen sun . . .

> . . . and the abstract Sun will rise,
> One splendour of earth, seas and skies,
>   As all the parts unite,
> As the spirit peers through the eyes and ears
> And the joyful heart now sees and hears
>   All things as beauty bright!

> With what bliss the ear thereof will hear!
> With what joy the eye will see!

In the foreground of Botticelli's picture rejoicing angels embrace the now living martyrs while the vanquished Fiend scurries to a rocky lair in a vain attempt to escape eternal judgment. What new Earth is this but Cresswell's at the end of his *Voyage?*—

> When we all shall rise as drowned men rise . . .
>
> To the sunlit main we'll rise again,
>   But ere we turn for shore
> By day and night in the sun so bright
> And the large, round moon with a new delight
> We'll frisk and play, for we've put to flight
>   The Fiend who plagues us sore.

Botticelli's art attempts that synthesis of pagan Antiquity and Christendom that we find in Cresswell's too, of which the poet wrote that it was something he "wanted through all his being." Was he successful in this aim? Just as Botticelli's *Mystic Nativity*, because of all that it attempts to embrace, has a certain restlessness of composition and lacks some of the serene unity and grace of his *Spring* or the simplicity of his *Venus*, so Cresswell's *Voyage*, in attempting an ultimate statement, is not as successful as the more strictly limited range of *The Forest*. But who, while admiring the charming simplicity of the *Venus*, could be satisfied with less than the joyous vision of *The Mystic Nativity*? Remember, too, that Cresswell had for years to be his own Savonarola while none would heed him.

Who will lead us to the promised land of the new Heaven and the new Earth? Not, according to Cresswell, either of the opposing giants who today threaten to split the world between them; not help but disaster only can be expected from them.

> See now between what last alternatives
> We stand: brute force; and outworn liberty:
> The Beast whose paw now lies on Hungary, he
> Who to the Pole a growling permit gives;
> And she who in the last, long twilight lives
> Of Transatlantic sunset, even she
> Whose cloudless morning was Thermopylae,
> Now the mere toast of showmen, crooks and spivs.
> Are these now the World's arbiters, these two?

Has France no voice to make her spirit known?
Or by the Yankee Gorgon over-glared
Are France and England turned to lifeless stone?[7]

Now we are the willing slaves of sensation and revel in sense-
less machines; and, says Cresswell, "it's this blind and degenerate
faculty which is increasing all over the World every minute which
must eventually seize the machines and all other devices of power
and government. . . . Nothing can avert this; and then the end
will be near. The downfall of reason, of modern science, by means
of the increase of sensation, will be colossal and terrible."[8] Only
then shall we be forced to turn for help and comfort and guidance
to "beings through whom and by whom the divine meaning of
Nature shall again appear to Mankind, beings in whom Man's
faculties will once again be seen in harmony."
These are poets, and with their coming a new poetry will arise,
and a new being for all men. But, Cresswell warns us, we must
not confuse these poets with today's "little mannequins of the
fashions" nor tomorrow's poetry with our current "morbid aberrations." It is because of this absolute refusal to compromise that
Cresswell found himself rejected not only by the worldling and
the philistine but also by the self-appointed promoters of modern
Western art which Cresswell attacked as decadent and even as
evil. Many, while looking to the evolution of new forms of art,
claimed that Surrealism, Abstraction and so on, were developing
"movements" in art and poetry. Cresswell denied that they have
any generic relation to poetry and art. In a letter dated two weeks
before his death, his last writing on the subject, we see how unchanging were his views, how unrelenting his attack.

. . . the result of the aberrant [Surrealist] use of these media [words
or colours or sounds] is to perpetuate all contraries; and (what is still
further from their use as poetry and art) to aggravate their division
and contrariness. For instance, in respect of Abstract and Cubist 'art',
the result of the former is merely to isolate the abstract extreme, while
the result of the latter is merely to isolate the concrete extreme. Now
we know that, in Nature, as in human nature, abstract and concrete
are contraries; but we also know that they are not isolated and irrecon-
cilable contraries, since a thing which is concrete evokes associations
which are abstract, and a memory which is abstract recognises a thing
which is concrete. Always the one phenomenon evokes the other. It is

by means of such associations that the arts of poetry, painting and music unite these and all other contraries to be harmony, as I said. But in the case of Abstract and Cubist 'art', as with all other aberrations known as Anti-art—Dada, Surrealism, Non-tonality and the rest— the contraries are not only unreconciled, they are finally and totally estranged. In most cases the 'picture' or 'poem' or piece of 'music' explodes, so to speak, in one's face!

I am not here concerned to judge between Art and Anti-art. But if one be good and beautiful then the other must be evil and ugly. If one be admirable and sincere then the other must be contemptible and fraudulent, even in Reading. Let us decide which is which, and cherish the one and show a proper aversion for the other. Let us not keep confusing them. If we can't do this, then indeed we deserve that a World so misguided should likewise explode in our faces.[9]

In that passage about the contraries of abstract and concrete and their evoking of associations, and their uniting to be harmony, we have in brief what Cresswell maintains *is* art. And as an affirmation of his own outlook (and as though to make sure that, after the untypical imagery of *The Voyage of the Hurunui,* we need have no fear that his views *otherwise* have changed in the slightest) only a year before his death there appeared his last poem published by The Trireme Press, of which he writes in a brief introduction:

The Trireme Press exists to rescue English Poetry from the state of intellectual (and often nonsensical) profanity into which it fell in the second and third decades of this Century, in imitation of the World's capital of artifice and chicanery, Paris. From the nonsensical profanity Poetry can rescue itself, and nearly has. From the intellectual profanity it can be rescued, like a debased currency, only by a return to the gold standard of inspiration, or *enthusiasmos* (being divinely possessed) as the Greeks rightly called the true creative illumination. This THE TRIREME PRESS seeks to effect, sometimes by circulating what it hopes has at least some faint colour and small feeble ingredient of the timeless true gold. But it is a one-man endeavour financed wholly from the weekly wages of a solitary night-watchman, and urgently in need of even the smallest assistance.

The poem is titled *Zandvoorter Preludes—1,* and is apparently the first of a series which Cresswell planned but did not live to complete. It is about Zandvoort, a seaside place in Holland, which

Cresswell visited with a Dutch friend, Jan Abspoel, to whom the
poem is dedicated.

> Padvinders!
> Why are there no greedy screaming gulls
>   on your beautiful coast,
> No biting gnats, no flies crawling on
>   everything
> As in England on the other side of this
>   magical sea?
>
> Why are your apples and fruits here so
>   much larger and more delicious to
>   eat than there?
> Why are your sand-dunes so white and
>   soft, their woods of oak and poplar
>   so richly jewelled and inlaid
> At sunrise and sunset with dark red
>   rubies and golden lapis and much green
>   jade,
> And all day lit from above with glitter-
>   ing sapphires, and just sometimes a
>   passing gleam of sea-born mother-of-
>   pearl,
> With a man-made music of waters drowsily,
>   ceaselessly murmuring night and day?
>
> And why, oh why is there so much kind-
>   ness and love and forgiveness here,
> And an end of torment, and instant peace
>   and joy, after so much fasting and
>   prayer?
>
> It is because the Gods, the holy erotic
>   pagan Gods, the Heavenly pathfinders,
>   are here,
> Of whom I shall say more (if they will
>   that I shall, and if my senses can
>   endure this brightness)
> As befits their greatness and coming
>   glory and power.

This poem has a much freer measure, an easy flowing and
natural statement, the work of a poet who is now relaxed and

assured. All his life Cresswell was his most severe critic, seldom admitting that he had achieved more than a basic honesty of expression or "some small ingredient of the timeless true gold." He once wrote to his friend and fellow poet, Denis Glover,

> My weakness is to deal in poetic rather than in natural writing. For as you know, the poetic is never poetry, while the natural is always so, and if it is natural to the point of taking the mind by surprise, then it is great poetry. A perfect structure or comprehension gives a natural expression inevitably . . .[10]

We see the application of this maxim in the aptly named *Prelude.* There is something of this natural freedom and comprehension that Cresswell strove for; perhaps, even, more than what he deprecatingly would call "a small measure of true poetry." We notice that it contains in miniature the scene or picture that is the key to all Cresswell's work. The greedy gulls, of course, are the exploiters of Nature's coasts; the biting gnats are those bickering, bloodsucking business parasites that prey on society; the crawling flies, the spreading, polluting industrial scene which reduces men to insects.

But there is "a magic sea," a cleansing baptism; and on the other side of that sea Love is found after a time of "fasting and prayer"; penitential suffering borne willingly and as willingly offered to the Gods. And following this we have again a portrayal of the fruits and joys of the earthly paradise. Why? "It is because the Gods are here"; a final affirmation of the poet's lifelong message and assurance of their "coming glory and power," all contained naturally in a fresh and charming picture of the Zandvoort coast and of human love and forgiveness.

The prose and poetry put before the reader of this study are, for the most part, Cresswell's published work but, besides the *Thesis,* there is quite a store of unpublished verse and various drafts and fragments of poems. Likewise, there are essays and the texts of talks, and the many letters in which the poet elaborates on his view of life and poetry and in which he sometimes admires or criticizes the work of other writers. Selections of this material, which throws light on many other facets of Cresswell's personality, will no doubt one day be published. But I think it can be maintained that Cresswell's reputation does not *depend* on the philosophizing or on the beauty of the prose; the three major poetic works which we have considered, together with individual lyrics and sonnets, have strength enough and strange beauty enough to stand on their own. Of the literary critics who noticed Cresswell's poetry only Robert Chapman showed understanding of this. In his short essay on Cresswell Professor Chapman wrote:

What I wish to stress is that D'Arcy Cresswell fought his own way to this picture of the right relation within and between individuals, poetry and society. It is darkly there in his sonnet sequence, *Lyttelton Harbour*. Its clearest prose exposition was given in a printed lecture of 1935 called *Eena Deena Dynamo, or The Downfall of Modern Science*. And it sustains his two long poems—the verse play, *The Forest*, and his allegory, *The Voyage of the Hurunui*. D'Arcy Cresswell had something to say that he felt urgently and in these two poems he said it. Their virtue does not lie in their parts. There are flashes of intensity in occasional lines and images. But these, like the rest, grow larger in the context of the whole poem, just as wit in an argument grows by the force it lends to good sense. This is just what Cresswell aimed at. He wanted his poetry to lend the cumulative force of feeling to the entire exposition of a large idea.

Cresswell sacrificed all to his uncompromising view of poetry and to his progress as a poet; indeed, his life became poetry. In his ardent pleading for the recognition of the poetic in man and in society by means of a renewed faith in our senses, he often made statements that even some of his friends refused to take seriously. But it was precisely on those occasions that he was most serious. When he maintained that, to any *sensible* man, the Earth was obviously mainly flat and that the Sun could be seen to move above it, a friend asked what then did it prove when a ship sailed away to the West and returned again from the East? Cresswell replied that that proved only how fond men are of their homes. Which reply was greeted with great laughter as though it were something extraordinarily witty. But, if one reflects, it is a simple and true reply. Far from trying to turn away awkward questions with a show of easy wit, as is the intellectual fashion nowadays, Cresswell uttered only what he meant. Yet he never lacked humor—especially when the joke was against himself. In proof of this, one has only to read many passages in *Present Without Leave*: for example, the story of his being captured as a spy

by United States forces at Panama and how, when he claimed
to be a poet, the Commandant thought he said pirate and had
him marched off under guard; or the consternation he caused
when, paying a formal call on the Governor-general, he made
a noisy assault on the locked main portals of Auckland's Government House instead of meekly following the sign that pointed
to a side door for public callers. Or, in a lengthy passage in
Margaret McMillan, the enjoyment with which he tells of what
happened when Lady Harknett in her mansion in London patron-
ized the French anarchist, La Vierge Rouge.

He was by nature gay, lively, and generous, and he was in-
tensely interested in every activity of mankind. All who knew him
will admit that he had talents which, had he wished (as often he
must have been tempted) to exploit, he could have made a name
as actor or novelist, painter or musician. But he channeled all
these considerable talents into the service of Poetry. To paraphrase
the last lines of *Lyttelton Harbour,* though the rough years drove
him onward he knew one light before him as behind, and his
conscience kept one course. So it is only fitting to end this study
by adapting, in respect of him, the words he wrote in praise of
a very kindred spirit, Margaret McMillan.

He neglected his talents in the pursuit of his genius, as all have the
duty, but few the courage, to do; and was rewarded, as all such are
rewarded, with the supreme felicity of dying free of all earthly ties and
with no regrets. Such take with them only what they wish to take, and
leave behind them only what they wish to leave.

Notes and References

[Verse preceding Introduction is from letter to Dr. T. T. Apsimon, June 2, 1958.]

Chapter One

1. *Eena Deena Dynamo*, preface.
2. Romans, 1:20 (Jerusalem Bible).
3. *Present Without Leave*, XLV.
4. *Our Life in This Land*, an essay by Roderick Finlayson, pp. 7–8
5. *Present Without Leave*, XII.
6. *Poems 1921–1927*.
7. "D'Arcy Cresswell, by his Friends," *Landfall* 56, Vol. 14 No. 4 (December 1960), p. 343.
8. *The Poet's Progress*, III.
9. *Ibid.*, VI.
10. *Ibid.*, XXXIX.
11. *Ibid.*, XXXIV.
12. *Ibid.*, XXXVII.
13. *Present Without Leave*, III.
14. *Ibid.*, III.
15. *Margaret McMillan*, pp. 153–154.
16. *Present Without Leave*, VI.
17. "The Decline of Taste," Cresswell papers, Auckland Public Library.
18. *Ibid.*
19. *Modern Poetry and the Ideal*, p. 17.
20. *Present Without Leave*, LIX.
21. *Ibid.*
22. *Margaret McMillan*, pp. 21–22. Italics added.
23. *Ibid.*, p. 53.
24. *Ibid.*, pp. 103–104.
25. *Ibid.*, p. 121.
26. *Ibid.*

Chapter Two

1. *The Poet's Progress,* II.
2. *Present Without Leave,* CI.
3. *The Poet's Progress,* VII.
4. *Ibid.,* XXIII.
5. *Ibid.*
6. See 1 Samuel 18:1–3: "After David had finished talking to Saul, Jonathan's soul became closely bound to David's and Jonathan came to love him as his own soul. Saul kept him by him from that day forward and would not let him go back to his father's house. Jonathan made a pact with David to love him as his own soul."
Also 2 Samuel 1: 26 (on the occasion of Jonathan's death): "I am desolate for you, Jonathan my brother. Very dear to me you were, your love to me more wonderful than the love of a woman."
Such love between men was considered natural then.
7. *Poems 1921–1927.* It would seem that Cresswell's decision, for the reason given in this sonnet, to leave his wife soon after their marriage is what he refers to in *The Poet's Progress* when he writes, "my private affairs just now were so tragic and cruel I had wished I were dead. . . . Now at last I knew what a price is paid for the purest art." He does not elaborate. Cresswell maintained that the private affairs of a public man should never become the concern of the public—as today decadent "publicity" wishes to make them. He also maintained that generally it were better for poets, as for priests, to lead a celibate life. On occasions after his 1938 return to England Cresswell was to meet his then grown son David.
8. *The Poet's Progress,* XXXIII.
9. *Poems 1924–1931.*
10. *Ibid.*
11. *The Poet's Progress,* XLVI.
12. *Present Without Leave,* LXXXII.
13. *The Poet's Progress,* XC.
14. *Ibid.,* XCIX.

Chapter Three

1. *Modern Poetry and the Ideal,* p. 8.
2. From D. H. Lawrence's introduction to his translation of *Cavalleria Rusticana,* Verga's stories of Sicilian peasants.
3. *Modern Poetry and the Ideal,* p. 17.
4. *Present Without Leave,* CLXXVI.
5. "In Spring" was first published October 14, 1936, in the lively Christchurch fortnightly *Tomorrow* edited by Kennaway Henderson.

6. Allen Curnow in the introduction to his *Book of New Zealand Verse*, Christchurch: The Caxton Press, 1945.

7. *Present Without Leave*, CLXXXIV.

8. This and the following quotations are from *Present Without Leave*, sections CXCVI, CXCVIII, CCL, CCIX respectively.

9. This and the following quotations up to the end of III are from typescript left by Cresswell with the author of this study. Some parts appeared as newspaper articles, some were read on the radio, some remained unpublished. Now among the Cresswell papers in the Auckland Public Library.

10. *Eena Deena Dynamo*, chapter 3.

11. *Ibid.*, chapter 6.

12. *Ibid.*, chapter 8.

13. *Ibid.*, chapter 10.

Chapter Four

1. These and the following lines are from "Invocation to Apollo."

2. The play, very slightly abridged, was presented in the Auckland Art Gallery in the winter of 1963 by Frank Sargeson and the New Independent Theatre Players, the producer being Christopher Cathcart. It ran for a week to small but enthusiastic audiences, thus confounding some critics who had claimed that the work was unplayable.

3. Matthew 13: 14–15 (Jerusalem Bible).

Chapter Five

1. Compare the neglect of Cresswell by his countrymen with the respect in which a writer like Bret Harte was held in America a century earlier. When in his early middle years Harte lacked a secure position, no one queried was his achievement great or his works immortal, but he was appointed United States Consul first to a town in Germany and later to Glasgow, with a vice-consul to do most of the routine work and at a salary that enabled him to support in comfort his family in America, and allowed him to indulge his fondness for elegant living and frequent travel. All this at a time when his country was still recovering from a civil war.

2. These and all the other stanzas in this chapter are from *The Voyage of the Hurunui*.

3. Compare this with "the pitch black sail of coming Chaos."

4. Alastair Campbell in *Landfall*, Vol. 10, No. 4, pp. 356–58, December 1956.

5. Keith Sinclair in *Landfall*, Vol. 6, No. 4, pp. 328–30, December 1952.

Chapter Six

1. In a letter to Ruth and Roderick Finlayson, August 27, 1950; Cresswell letters, Auckland Public Library.

2. In a letter to Dr. T. T. Apsimon, December 16, 1959; *Letters of D'Arcy Cresswell*, edited by Helen Shaw. Accusing Dr. Apsimon of being blind to the value of the poetry because of disapproval of the manner of the poet's life, Cresswell wrote to him, "Were the above [poem] a translation of Sappho, from the Greek, you would have accepted its survival without question, without a qualm about Lesbianism and the mis-spent life. . . ."

3. In a letter to Dr. T. T. Apsimon, June 1958; *Letters of D'Arcy Cresswell.*

4. Alone among critics in his insight regarding Cresswell's work, Robert Chapman wrote: "D'Arcy Cresswell spent his life seeking, finding and expressing one major insight or complex idea. As a poet he was an original in taking a drastic and unchanging course." From a short essay on "The Work of D'Arcy Cresswell," *Image* No. 7 (1960), pp. 1–2.

5. From a letter to Ursula Bethell, August, 1934; *Letters of D'Arcy Cresswell.*

6. From a letter to J. H. E. Schroder, September, 1933; also in *The Letters.* In the light of these earlier letters it is interesting to recall that in 1942 Cresswell was formally confirmed as a Christian. That rite took place in the Church of England; but more than once Cresswell expressed to the present author his belief that the Roman Catholic Church had kept the truer faith. His choosing to be confirmed in the Church of England could be viewed as merely loyalty to family tradition, but perhaps we could see it as a harbinger of the present spirit of ecumenism. In any case, he said later that he had soon returned to the path he began to tread as a small child when he listened to the voices of sea and wind and earth and sky that spoke with him. "That was my true communion, and bread and wine. . . ."

7. *After Suez,* a poem that Cresswell sent to some of his friends to be added to their copies of the *Cyprus Sonnets.*

8. *Eena Deena Dynamo,* chapter 10.

9. Draft letter to Professor A. G. Lehmann, February 8, 1960 (only a week or two before Cresswell's death); in the Turnbull Library, Wellington.

10. In the Turnbull Library, Wellington.

Selected Bibliography

1. *Primary Sources: Writings by Cresswell.*

A. *Poetry:*
Poems 1921–1927. London: Gardner and Darton, 1927.
Poems 1924–1931. London: The Bodley Head, 1931.
Lyttelton Harbour. Auckland: The Unicorn Press, 1936.
The Forest. Auckland: The Pelorus Press, 1952.
The Voyage of the Hurunui. Christchurch: The Caxton Press, 1956.
Poems for Poppycock. London: The Trireme Press, 1957.
Poetry and Cyprus. London: The Trireme Press, 1957.
Leander: an Elegy. London: The Trireme Press, 1958.
More Poetry for Poppycock. London: The Trireme Press, 1959.
Zandvoorter Preludes—. London: The Trireme Press, 1959.

B. *Prose:*
The Poet's Progress. London: Faber and Faber, 1930.
Modern Poetry and the Ideal. Auckland: The Griffin Press, 1934.
Eena Deena Dynamo. Christchurch: The Caxton Press, 1936.
Present Without Leave. London: Cassell and Co., 1939.
Margaret McMillan. London: Hutchinson and Co., 1948.
The Thesis on the Mechanism of Spirit and Poetic Intention in Man, typescript copies of this and other essays and papers and letters in the Auckland Public Library and the Turnbull Library, Wellington. Undated.
The Letters of D'Arcy Cresswell, edited by Helen Shaw. Christchurch: Canterbury University Press, 1971.

2. *Secondary Sources: Writings on Cresswell Cited in the Text.*
Campbell, Alastair, review of *The Voyage of the Hurunui. Landfall* 10, 4 (December 1956), pp. 356–58.
Chapman, Robert, "The Work of D'Arcy Cresswell." *Image* No. 7 (1960), pp. 1–2.
Curnow, Allen, *A Book of New Zealand Verse 1923–45.* Christchurch: Caxton Press, 1945.
"D'Arcy Cresswell, by his friends." *Landfall* 14, 4 (December 1960), pp. 341–63.
Sinclair, Keith, review of *The Forest. Landfall* 6, 4 (December 1952), pp. 328–30.

Index